An Illustrated History of Music for Young Musicians

THE MIDDLE AGES AND THE RENAISSANCE

Gilles Comeau
Rosemary Covert

Thanks

The authors and publisher wish to thank the people in charge of the libraries, museums, galleries and private collections named below, for permitting the reproduction of works of art in their collections.

A.F. Kersting; Abtei St. Hildegard; AKG, London; Alinari/Art Resource, New York; Allan Dean Walker, Santa Monica; Austrian National Library; Bayerische Staatsbibliothek, Munich; BBC Hulton Picture Library; Biblioteca Ambrosiana, Milan; Bibliothèque Nationale, Paris; Bibliothèque Royale, Brussel; Bildarchiv der. Ost. Nationalbibliothek; British Library, London; British Museum, London; Bulloz; Canali Photobank, Milan; Château de Fontainebleau; Church of the Eremitani, Padua; Corbis/Bettman; Dagli Orti, Paris; Éditions Alphonse Leduc, Paris; Explorer Archives, Vanves; Fitzwilliam Museum, Cambridge; Frichi Arborio Mella Calcaterra, Milan; Galleria degli Uffizi, Florence; Galleria dell'Accademia, Florence; Galleria Nazionale d'Arte Antica, Rome; Giancarlo Costa, Milan; Giraudon; Heidelberg University Library; Hermitage, St. Petersburg; Index Florence; Italian Government Tourist Office; Kunsthistorisches Museum, Vienna; Metropolitan Museum of Art; Monastery of the Escorial, Madrid; Musée cantonal des Beaux-Arts, Lausanne; Musée Condé, Chantilly; Musée du Berry, Bourges; Musée de Blois; Musée de Versailles; Musée des Beaux-Arts, Lille; Musée du Louvre, Paris; Museo Correr, Venice; Museo del Prado, Madrid; Museo dell' Opera del Duomo, Siena; Museo Nazionale del Bargello; National Gallery, London; National Museums and Galleries on Merseyside; National Portrait Gallery, London; Osterreichische Nationalbibliothek, Vienna; Palazzo Publico, Siena; Pinacoteca Communale Volterra; Prado, Madrid; RMN, Paris; S. Francesco, Arezzo; S. Giorgio Maggiore, Venice; S. Pietro in Vincoli, Rome; S. Tomé, Toledo, Spain; Scala/Art Resource, New York; Schloss Harrach, Rohrau; Santa Maria del Carmine, Florence; Santa Maria delle Grazie, Milan; Stadt-und Universitatsbibliothek, Frankfurt; Stanza della Segnatura, Vatican Palace; Thames and Hudson; The Lebrecht Collection, London; The Mansell Collection; The Royal Collection, Her Majecty Queen Elizabeth II; The Vatican, Rome; University of California at Berkeley Music Library; Victoria and Albert Museum; Viscount L'Isle Collection.

Cover & design:	Martine Mongrain and Marie-Josée Hotte
Printer:	Centre franco-ontarien de ressources pédagogiques

© CFORP, 2000
    290 Dupuis Street, Vanier, Ontario K1L 1A2
      Phone orders: (613) 747-1553
        Fax: (613) 747-0866
      Web site: http://www.cforp.on.ca
      E-mail: cforp@cforp.on.ca

All rights reserved.

No part of this book may be reproduced or transmitted in any form or by any means, electronic, mechanical, photocopying, recording, or otherwise, without permission in writing from the Publisher.

Every reasonable care has been taken to trace and acknowledge ownership of copyright material. The Publisher welcomes information that might rectify any errors or omissions.

ISBN 2-89442-557-0
Copyright — second semester 2000
National Library of Canada
           Printed in Canada

PREFACE

To modern readers in the 21st century, the Middle Ages and the Renaissance seem very far away—so remote, in fact, that we may feel nothing in common with the people or the life in those different times. *An Illustrated History of Music for Young Musicians: The Middle Ages and the Renaissance* beckons us into this fascinating world of 1 000 years ago and succeeds in performing the impossible. We are transported back in history, the antique becomes current, and we too are there, fighting in the Mediaeval Crusades or witnessing Michelangelo's sculpture of David come to life in the Renaissance.

History is a story—a good story—and everyone loves a story, especially a good one. The authors of this book are master storytellers who weave a riveting tale. Readers receive much more than mere facts, although there are plenty of those. We are treated to the flavour of these eras in a detailed but easily accessible manner. The highly descriptive language prevents typical "dry-history-text" syndrome. The reader may know very little about these times, but is gently led through history from the specific ("How the Peasant Lived") to the abstract ("Harmony") in an anecdotal, rather than academic manner, as if spoken to, rather than lectured. The esoteric concept of the development of harmony, for example, is explained clearly; the end of modality leading to the supremacy of tonality is outlined in a very natural, easily grasped manner.

History is presented in a continuous line, the Middle Ages moving smoothly to the Renaissance. Before us parades a panorama of fascinating people, the real people of history: Joan of Arc, Guinevere and Lancelot, Shakespeare. This is music history as history first and foremost. Once the authors have set the rich background of each era, filled in details of the social customs, politics, sciences, literature, theatre, architecture, paintings and decorative arts—then, and only then, does the music become the focus. The reader is ready, armed with the background knowledge to understand that most ephemeral of the arts, music.

A good history text should pique the curiosity and intrigue the reader enough to search further. *An Illustrated History of Music for Young Musicians: The Middle Ages and the Renaissance* provides an expertly guided tour, which whets the appetite for more. The lives and music of the finest composers of each era are explored. For each composer, we are provided with suggestions of his or her most representative works… and we are left with a hunger to hear them.

The book refers to that great humanist thinker of the Renaissance, Erasmus, who "held enlightened views about education and teaching children… and encouraged arousing the children's interest." Having read this book, I feel Erasmus would be pleased.

Clayton C. Scott, pianist, teacher, workshop clinician
Board of Examiners, Royal Conservatory of Music of Toronto (Music History, Harmony)

Table of Contents

The History of Music

The Middle Ages

Introduction 7

Life in the Middle Ages 8
    The Political Situation 8
    Society and Culture 16
    Science 26

The Arts in the Middle Ages 28
    Literature 28
    Architecture 31
    Painting and Decorative Arts 34
    Sculpture 38

Musical Life in the Middle Ages 40
    The Church 40
    The Court 42

Music in the Middle Ages

Characteristics of Music in the Middle Ages 44
    General Features 44
    Specific Features 46

Composers 54

The Renaissance

Introduction 57

Life in the Renaissance 58
    The Political Situation 58
    Society and Culture 63
    Science and Thought 70

The Arts in the Renaissance 74
    Literature 74
    Architecture 76
    Sculpture 78
    Painting 80

Musical Life in the Renaissance 88
    Professional Musicians 88
    Amateur Musicians 90

Music in the Renaissance

Characteristics of Renaissance Music 91
    General Features 91
    Specific Features 92
    Liturgical Forms 95
    Secular Forms 97
    Instrumental Music 99
    Instrumental Forms 100

Composers 101
    Early Renaissance 101
    High Renaissance 104

The History of Music

Over the years, music in the Western world has been changing constantly and the music of today is very different from the music people made 300 years ago.

To help you understand how this music has developed, each of the books in this series will describe a different musical period. For each era, we will show you the way the people of the time lived, and the kinds of art and architecture that were typical of the period. We will discuss the important musical characteristics and describe the lives and contributions of the major composers.

The history of Western music is usually divided into six broad time periods:

Middle Ages	Renaissance	Baroque	Classical	Romantic	Twentieth Century
	1450	1600	1750	1825	1900

The first half of this book presents the Middle Ages.

The Middle Ages

It is generally agreed that the Middle Ages began more or less in the fifth century, after the fall of the western part of Roman Empire, and lasted until the beginning of the Renaissance in the fifteenth to sixteenth century, depending on the location. Later scholars looking back on the time called these 1 000 or so years the Middle Ages because they thought that they marked a time of stagnation between two great civilizations. Modern historians, however, recognize that the Middle Ages were a period of great change and that the events and ideas of the period have been the foundation of many of our modern institutions.

Life in the Middle Ages

The Political Situation

From tribal groups to kingdoms

After the collapse of the Roman Empire, the territory that is now called Europe and the British Isles was in the hands of a number of different people. The Franks, a Germanic tribe, held sway in what is now France and Germany, the Anglo-Saxons had England, the Celts were primarily in Ireland. Organization was local, and trade and commerce almost died out. The first group to become something like a state were the Franks, whose king, Clovis I, converted to Christianity in 496. Historians regard Clovis as the first King of France.

Justinian I, ruler of the Byzantine Empire (527-565)

The Roman Empire was divided into eastern and western portions in the late third century. The western portion collapsed, but the eastern empire, centred in Constantinople, the site of the ancient city of Byzantium, dominated the Mediterranean world.

Charlemagne was a strong believer in civilization. He collected books written in Latin left behind by the Romans and had them copied. He encouraged education and tried to establish the rule of law.

A sculpture of the head of Charlemagne

The empire of the Franks reached its peak under Charlemagne who became king in 768. In 800, he was crowned the ruler of a huge territory that stretched across most of Europe. After his death, however, the empire was divided up among his sons. The western portion became the basis for what is now France, and the eastern lands ultimately became Germany.

The crowning of Charlemagne

This illumination shows Charlemagne seated, his power symbolized by the sword.

8 The Middle Ages

The Political Situation

Life in the Middle Ages

From tribal groups to kingdoms

From about 800 to 1100, people from Scandinavia known as the Vikings raided the shores of Europe and the British Isles. They were ferocious warriors, settling in the lands they conquered. Over time they too converted to Christianity, and became farmers and traders as well as warriors. Viking invaders were given the territory of Normandy in 911, and 150 years later, in 1066, William, Duke of Normandy, crossed the channel separating England and France and claimed the crown of England. He slew the Saxon king, Harold, at the Battle of Hastings and was crowned king at Westminster Abbey.

For the rest of the medieval period, there were struggles for territory between the various powerful royal dynasties of the European continent and the British Isles. Territories were gained by marriage and lost and won in wars.

The hull of a Viking sailing ship on display in a museum in Oslo.

A detail from the Bayeux tapestry showing Norman knights charging in the Battle of Hastings

The Middle Ages

Life in the Middle Ages

The Political Situation

Feudalism

Feudalism was a system of political organization that governed everyone's role in society. The mediaeval world was divided into nobility, clergy and peasants, and the feudal system was based on a series of contracts between the nobles. It was closely linked to the manorial or seigneurial system, which governed the relationship between those who owned land and those who worked it.

In general, all land was owned by the king. The king granted land, called fiefs, to various noblemen in return for military service. The noble promised to be the king's vassal, or servant, and swore an oath of fealty to his lord. The lord had to protect the vassal, and the vassal had to provide a specified number of warriors whenever the lord wanted them. Important noblemen, like the barons, had large fiefs, which they could subdivide, and they could themselves grant fiefs to lords lower in the hierarchy, who would in turn owe them military service.

The feudal system enabled armies to be mustered when needed without large standing armies having to be maintained, although in the later Middle Ages, when vassals could pay "shield money" instead of supplying knights, it was possible for kings, for instance, to maintain a force of mercenary soldiers. Feudalism was also a way of ensuring loyalty, by binding knights to an overlord.

In society's second rank, the clergy, the most important men were the archbishops and bishops. Archbishops were often advisors to kings and played an important role in the politics of the day. The bishops could be as powerful as the barons. Each bishop ruled over a diocese and all the churches and monasteries within its boundaries. Villagers and peasants had to pay one tenth of everything they produced to the church, so bishops could become very rich through the collection of these tithes.

William the Conqueror built this stone stronghold in London after he became king. It was guarded by stone walls and a moat that filled from the Thames River. It is the oldest part of the still-standing Tower of London.

This manuscript illustration shows the King of France and his court. Seated below the king are the upper nobility, the barons on his left, and the bishops wearing their mitres. Below them, standing, are all the lesser nobles.

10   The Middle Ages

The Political Situation

Life in the Middle Ages

The seigneurial system

The seigneurial or manorial system describes the relationship between the landowners and the people who worked the land. Land belonged to the nobility. Each estate had a lord of the manor, or seigneur, and the land was worked by the peasants who lived in the village that was part of the estate. The lord had to protect the peasants and he administered justice in the manorial courts. The land was divided up into arable land, which could support crops; pasture land, called the commons, where all the people had a right to graze their animals; and woodlands, where the lord alone had the right to hunt. The arable land was divided into strips and each peasant held one or more strips. He could farm these for his own use, but he also had to work for the lord one or more days a week, perhaps more in the busy season. He also had to have his grain ground in the lord's mills and baked into bread in the lord's ovens and pay for the privilege.

There were two kinds of peasants, the free and the servile. The free peasants tended to be the village craftsmen, and the servile ones the agricultural workers or serfs. In exchange for working the lord's land, the serfs were generally given a rough dwelling, some strips of land, a few animals and the right to pasture them. What distinguishes serfs from slaves is that they had the right to hold the land and leave it to their descendants, even if the manor changed hands. They could not be sold as property, and in theory could buy their freedom from the lord.

This illustration shows the timber-framed huts of dried mud and plaster that were common peasant dwellings. Often animals and people shared the same roof. Here, the sheep are being let out to graze the pasture land.

The Middle Ages

The Church

When Pope Leo III crowned Charlemagne ruler of the Holy Roman Empire on Christmas Day, 800, he set a precedent lasting for several hundred years that said the popes had the right to select, crown and perhaps even get rid of kings and emperors.

The Christian religion originated in the Near East, but by the time the Roman Empire collapsed in the middle of the fifth century, it had spread all around the Mediterranean area and throughout Europe, its influence stretching from Ireland to Ethiopia. As the Germanic tribes invaded, their leaders converted, so that in a time when political affiliations were very loose, the Church was almost universal. The Western branch of the Church was headed by the Bishop of Rome, called the Pope. The Pope was chosen by the clergy in Rome and his power was absolute. The popes had a great deal of influence over the kings and rulers of the various tribes, and could excommunicate anyone who did not behave. Pope Leo III crowned Charlemagne ruler of the Holy Roman Empire, the largest in Europe. Pope Gregory VII excommunicated Emperor Henry IV over a struggle for power, and Henry had to dress in rags to beg for forgiveness.

At the peak of its power in the twelfth and thirteenth centuries, the Church was the most proficient administrative and governing organization in Western Europe. It was also one of the richest. It had its own laws and its own courts, and owned a great deal of property. Catholicism was the only religion in Europe and it ruled almost every facet of people's lives, from birth to death.

This tapestry shows the splendour and influence of the church, as the bishop blesses a nobleman who is preparing to leave on crusade.

A dinner that included a king, a duke, the Pope and several bishops

The Church

One of the reasons for the spread of the Church was the monastic system. Monastic orders, communities of monks or nuns, dispersed throughout Europe, building abbeys and becoming centres of learning and culture, as well as giving aid to the secular communities that were growing up around them. The language of the Church was Latin, and the clergy were responsible for preserving what written records were left of the Roman Empire and its culture, as well as that of other ancient civilizations, like the Greeks and the Etruscans. The writings of Roman writers like Virgil, Ovid and Cicero were preserved by the monks working in the scriptoria, or writing rooms, of the monasteries. The Church established the first schools, which educated both young people entering the Church as well as laymen.

St. Benedict and his monks feeding the poor

The oldest monastic order was that of St. Benedict, who founded the first Western monastery in Monte Cassino in the sixth century. The monks had to follow the Benedictine Rule, by which they took vows of poverty, chastity and obedience. Monasteries and abbeys all over Europe came to live by the Rule. By the tenth century, many felt that the monastic life had become too lax. Other orders were formed, such as the one at Cluny, whose members returned to a strict adherence to the rules set down by St. Benedict. In 1115, St. Bernard of Clairvaux formed an order of reformed Benedictines called the Cistercians, who were the most influential order in the twelfth century. The Franciscan order, named after St. Francis of Assisi, who dedicated his life to prea-ching to the poor, did not live in monasteries, but went from community to community, preaching to the poor and begging for food.

St. Bernard of Clairvaux

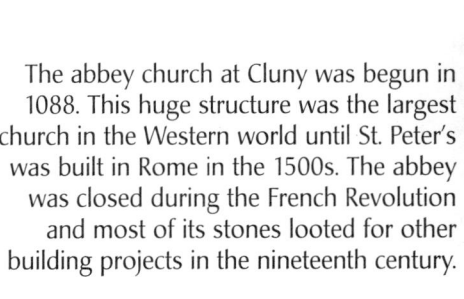

The abbey church at Cluny was begun in 1088. This huge structure was the largest church in the Western world until St. Peter's was built in Rome in the 1500s. The abbey was closed during the French Revolution and most of its stones looted for other building projects in the nineteenth century.

St. Francis is always associated with love for animals and birds.

The Crusades

Urban II preaching about sending a crusade to the Holy Land at Clermont in 1095

Pilgrimages to the Holy Land where Jesus Christ had lived and died were traditional for pious Christians. The Holy Land was under Muslim rule, but they tolerated pilgrims and the Church could tolerate their authority. However, in the eleventh century the Muslims began to refuse to allow pilgrims to enter. In 1095, Pope Urban II called for a holy war to recapture Jerusalem, the site of the Crucifixion. Different groups with different noble leaders from across Europe marched to Constantinople, where they met and continued on to lay siege to Jerusalem. The Christian forces were victorious, after a bloody and destructive battle, which included the massacre of many of the local people. Many of the victorious knights saw this as an opportunity to set up feudal states to protect the routes to the Christian holy sites as well as to make their own fortunes. Four Crusader states were established, including the Kingdom of Jerusalem, whose ruler was Godefroi de Bouillon, a French nobleman. Many castles and fortifications were built in the Crusader states to protect them from the Muslims. There were seven major Crusades to repel Muslim attacks over the next 200 years, but in the end the Muslims gradually recaptured the territory. Christian rule ended with the fall of the city of Acre in 1291.

After Godefroi de Bouillon died, his brother Baldwin was crowned King of Jerusalem.

The mediaeval fortress of Krak des Chevaliers, in Syria on the northern Lebanese border, still stands. It was built in 1142 by the military monastic order of the Knights Hospitallers.

This manuscript illustration shows the King of France going on a crusade.

The Political Situation

The growth of trade

The Crusades may not have been a military success in the long term, but they were certainly an economic one. Sending such large forces such a long distance required skills that had all but died out since the Romans. Large sums of money were needed, supplies had to be produced and distributed, fleets of ships had to be amassed to transport people. Trade revived around the Mediterranean, and cities like Genoa, Venice and Marseilles became important centres. With the growth of cities, there was more need for trade in foodstuffs, and farmers learned to be more productive in response to this need.

Money came into circulation in the West again, after gold was rediscovered by the Crusaders, and mints were established. Banking had been discouraged by the Church, since lending money at interest was thought to be unchristian, but the need to finance trade brought in not only loans, but insurance and letters of credit. The adoption of Arabic numerals instead of Roman made commerce and banking much easier.

Sea trade was improved with the use of the compass, a Chinese invention adopted by the Muslims. Arab sailors had developed the rudder, which was fixed to the stern of the boat and controlled by a horizontal tiller, far easier to use than the traditional steering oar. These two developments made long-distance ocean voyages more possible. Trade goods began to move from place to place, bringing with them new ideas and exposure to other cultures. England exported wool and tin, France honey and wine. Flanders traded in cloth, Russia in furs. A few Europeans, like Marco Polo in 1295, travelled as far as China, bringing back spices, silk and perfume.

Pilgrims bound for the Holy Land had to get to Venice first, and then cross the Mediterranean by ship. They usually purchased what they needed for the voyage in Venice, which was very good for the economy of that city.

Life in the Middle Ages — Society and Culture

How the nobility lived

The properties owned by the nobles varied from castles with huge estates to simple manor houses with a modest fief. A very rich person might own several estates in different places. Their lives varied too according to their station, but their values and activities would be similar.

The lord had a duty to run the business of his property, and to make decisions about all the people on his manor. He also had to serve his king in court and on the battlefield, so he often had a steward to manage his affairs while he was away, to collect the taxes and make decisions. His lady was responsible for overseeing the servants, the cooks and the kitchen, and for entertaining guests. Often wives stepped in and took over their husbands' duties when they were away fighting. Generally the nobility had possessions that were suited to their high social position. They wore clothes made of fine fabrics, jewellery, and their homes, whether castle or manor house, were made of stone, with beds to sleep in and fine hangings to keep out the drafts.

This castle, the Château de Fougères in northwest France, would probably have protected the entire village.

Not all of the nobility lived in castles. This fortified manor house is an example of a more modest residence for one of the lesser nobility.

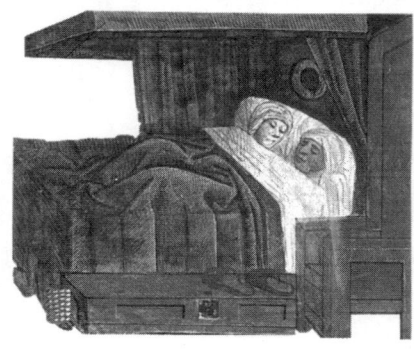

This illustration from a mediaeval book shows a bed in a well-to-do household, with canopy and draperies to keep out the cold.

The lord is wearing a short tunic or doublet over a pair of hose, or stockings. The lady's dress is fitted at the waist and most of its fullness is in the front. Tall headdresses were fashionable, sometimes with a veil attached. Ladies never displayed their ankles.

16 The Middle Ages

Society and Culture

Life in the Middle Ages

How the nobility lived

The lord and his court spent a great deal of their time hunting, which was both a sport and a necessity, for it provided the meat for the lord's table. They would hunt deer or wild boar from horseback with a pack of hounds to locate the prey, or they would hunt with trained falcons, fierce birds of prey trained to kill small game like birds and rabbits and then return to their masters. Both men and women enjoyed playing board games like chess, checkers and backgammon. Women did needlework for practical reasons, as well as to create something beautiful, and reading aloud was an important activity when such a small percentage of the population could actually read. Listening to stories and then telling them to others was an important way of passing on the culture. Music, like singing or playing the lute, was also an important accomplishment.

This tapestry shows a noble lady being read to as she spins thread.

An illustration from the *Très Riches Heures du duc de Berry*, a famous mediaeval manuscript. Here we see the Duke dining.

A hunting party
This is another picture from the *Très Riches Heures du duc de Berry*.

This wood carving shows a mediaeval couple playing chess with two onlookers.

The Middle Ages 17

Life in the Middle Ages

Society and Culture

Becoming a knight

Mediaeval society was essentially organized around war. The feudal structure was set up in response to the need for mounted knights to fight wars for the king. To become a knight, a boy had to serve a long apprenticeship. Sons of the nobility were sent to become pages in a knight's household. As teenagers, they would become squires, and would look after their knight's horse and armour. They practised all the skills necessary to be a soldier and would gain actual experience in war. After performing a heroic deed on the battlefield, or more usually, simply by coming of age, the squire would be made a knight, being dubbed with a sword or slapped in the face by his lord. He also would be given his fief, or grant of land.

This picture shows a group of squires learning soldierly skills, like sword fighting, fighting with quarterstaves, throwing spears and wrestling.

Stone throwing
Spear throwing
Acrobatics
Sword-fighting
Wrestling
Fighting with quarterstaves

Arms and armour

In the early Middle Ages, the most common weapons were lances and swords, and for protection the knight wore a helmet, and a tunic called a hauberk made of leather or quilted cloth. Later the hauberks were made of mail, metal rings that were joined together to form a fabric that almost looked as if it were knitted. A cloth tunic carrying the knight's coat of arms was worn over the mail, and he also had a shield to protect against battle axes. Having his coat of arms emblazoned on his tunic and shield helped identify a helmeted knight in battle. In the early 1300s, crossbows became so much improved that they could easily shoot through the mail hauberk, so plate armour was invented. Steel plates were fastened to the mail to cover the chest and back, shoulders, and the outside surface of the arms and legs.

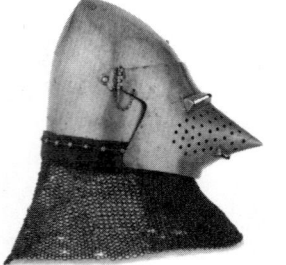

A helmet with mail collar from the end of the 1300s

This knight is wearing mail all over, topped by a surcoat with his arms.

A full suit of plate armour

18 The Middle Ages

Society and Culture

Life in the Middle Ages

War games

In the early Middle Ages, tournaments were a way of training knights for battle. Later, when kings were employing trained mercenaries, tournaments became a form of entertainment for the court and a way for knights to demonstrate their skills, the way athletes do today. There were different kinds of combat. The mêlée pitted teams of knights against each other in a simulated battle. Jousting was single combat, where two knights rode at each other and tried to unhorse their opponent with a lance. Sometimes they continued to fight on foot, with swords.

The code of chivalry

The code of chivalry began with the expectation that a knight would be brave and loyal to his lord. Over time, the notion came to include religious piety, under the influence of the crusades. Knights were not supposed to attack unarmed people nor fight for monetary gain. They should treat their fellow knights and social inferiors respectfully. The notion of courtly love also affected the code of chivalry. A knight was expected to dedicate himself to a noble woman, one who was betrothed or married to another, and he fought in her name and tried to win her favour in tournaments. The arts were an important part of courtly love; knights had to write poetry, sing love songs and play musical instruments as a way of pleasing their lady. By the end of the Middle Ages, when nation-states were becoming more important than feudal relationships, and kings were more likely to hire mercenary soldiers, the knights' role became less practical and more symbolic. The values of chivalry became more a mark of nobility and social distinction.

These two knights are jousting at a tournament held by King Edward III of England in honour of the Countess of Salisbury.

These illustrations of knights jousting show the heraldic devices on their tunics, shields and horses.

This shield is decorated with a knight kneeling before his lady. The scroll reads "You or death," and behind the knight stands the figure of death.

The Middle Ages 19

Life in the Middle Ages

Society and Culture

How the peasants lived

Obtaining water is a problem not obvious to modern city dwellers but in mediaeval times, it could be very difficult. Running water in houses did not exist. People who lived in the country could get clean water from streams, and well-to-do people had wells, but poorer people in the city had to go and collect water from the fountain in their neighbourhood and carry it home.

These two peasants are separating out the fibre that made linen thread from dried flax.

This picture shows a carpenter using a brace and bit to drill holes in a piece of wood.

Peasants were either farmers or craftsmen. The farmers worked the land of their lord and also had to pay rent to the lord in crops from the harvest of their own land. They usually had two harvests a year. In the spring they would grow barley, oats, hay, peas and beans, and in the fall wheat and rye. The wheat and rye were ground into flour to make bread, the barley was used for beer and the hay and oats were used for animals. Peas and beans were dried and used for food. Farmers would join forces for plowing because few of them had enough oxen to do it themselves. They also learned from experience to rotate their crops and allow fields to lie fallow once every three years so that the soil would not be drained of all its nutrients.

Craftsmen were very important people in a mediaeval town. Millers ground grains into flour, bakers baked bread, blacksmiths made tools and shod horses, shoemakers and seamstresses provided footwear and clothes, candlemakers provided the possibility of light after the sun went down. Craftspeople generally learned their trade from their families or by being apprenticed to another skilled craftsperson for seven years.

Most peasants lived in rough, thatched-roof cottages and slept in their work clothes on straw-filled mattresses on the floor, with an animal skin for a blanket. Furniture would consist of benches, and a wooden chest in which they could store their possessions. They ate with wooden bowls, cups and spoons. Often their livestock lived in the house with them. Only better-off peasants would have woollen blankets and linen towels.

Here craftsmen are cutting stone, mixing mortar and building a church.

20 The Middle Ages

Society and Culture

Life in the Middle Ages

How the clergy lived

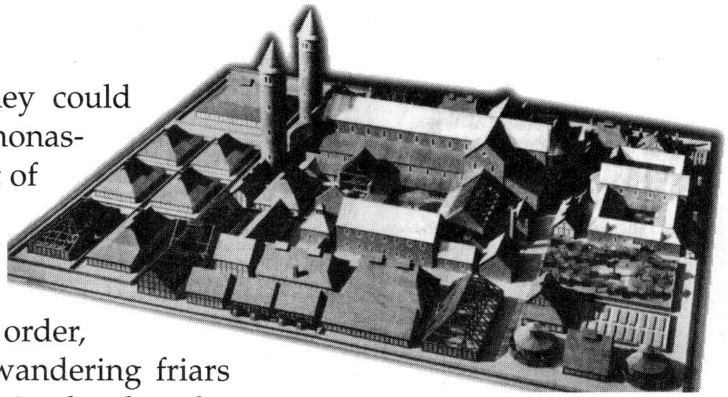

Both men and women joined the clergy. They could either live in a cloistered community like a monastery, an abbey, or a convent, or they could be part of a religious order that went out into the world to serve people. Those who went into a monastery withdrew from society so they could concentrate on prayer or scholarship, or depending on the order, healing the sick and preaching. Some became wandering friars who went from town to town preaching, others joined orders devoted to teaching.

Abbeys were the enclosed communities where groups of monks or nuns lived, ruled by an abbot or an abbess. An abbey would usually have a church, a dormitory in which each of the inhabitants would have their own small cell and a dining hall. Often there would be a library, a guesthouse for travellers, and perhaps an infirmary for the sick. There was usually a large courtyard bounded by a cloister, or secluded colonnade, where the clergy could walk without coming into contact with the secular world.

There were nine daily church services in an abbey or monastery, beginning as early as two or three o'clock in the morning. The monks or nuns did other work during the hours they were not in church. Many would work in the scriptorium, copying manuscripts, while others taught, or worked in the abbey's fields, kitchen or hospital. Some monasteries were famous for things they produced, like wine, beer, cheese or honey.

This is a model made from an 820 plan for a monastery. The largest building is the church, but included in the complex is a guest house, an infirmary, workshops, farm buildings and a cemetery planted with fruit trees.

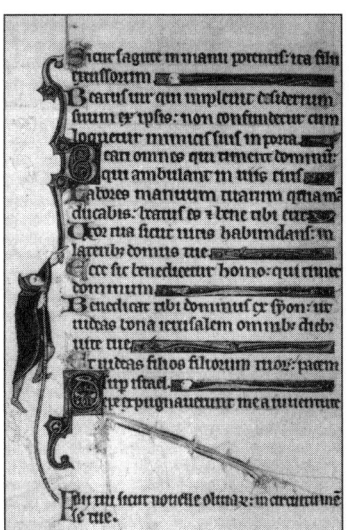

The scribe who copied out this illuminated page left out a line of the text. You can see where he has added it in at the bottom, and drawn a little person pointing to the place these words belong.

A religious service in a monastery is illustrated in this fifteenth century book of hours.

Two monks work at their desks copying manuscripts.

The Middle Ages

The Black Death

The Black Death, a form of bubonic plague, arrived in Western Europe in the fourteenth century. The plague is caused by bacteria that are spread by infected fleas and rats. It originated in China, and moved through the trade routes to the Middle East, first arriving in a ship that landed in Sicily in 1347. Over the next three years it swept through Europe and into Scandinavia. Twenty-five million Europeans died in the first wave. The disease returned five more times before the end of the century, killing a greater proportion of the population than any other disease or war in history.

Burying victims of the plague in 1349

Plague victims suffered from fever, chills, swollen lymph nodes and haemorrhages that turned black. It also affected the lungs, so was easily spread though coughing and sneezing. The plague still exists, but it is not usually fatal. In the Middle Ages, there was no medication that could combat it.

Life expectancy in the Middle Ages was very low, even without the Black Death. What with war, famine, leprosy, typhoid, rabies and countless other illnesses that were impossible to cure, the average adult lived only into his or her twenties. Infant mortality was extremely high.

This modern excavation of a fourteenth century cemetery in London shows a mass grave for victims of the 1348–49 plague. In spite of the crisis and the number of bodies that had to be dealt with, the orderliness of the remains suggest that the dead were still given a decent burial.

Society and Culture

Life in the Middle Ages

The Inquisition

Being a member of the Catholic Church was not optional in the Middle Ages. People who did not adhere to the official dogma of the Church of Rome were called heretics and could be tried in a church court and sentenced to a variety of punishments, including death. Often they were tortured to obtain a confession. The mediaeval Inquisition was established by the Pope in 1231 to eliminate some heretical sects in southern France. People who belonged to these sects were tortured and burned.

The Spanish Inquisition did not begin until 1478, when the Catholic powers there used it to eliminate Jews and Muslims from Spain. The Grand Inquisitor was the infamous Dominican monk Tomás de Torquemada, who employed torture and confiscation to terrify his victims. One of his practices was the public ceremony called the auto-da-fé. The prisoner would be conducted in a solemn procession to a public place where the death sentence would be pronounced and he or she would be burned at the stake.

One of the most famous heretics is Joan of Arc. Joan was a peasant girl who heard the voices of saints telling her that God wanted her to save France from the English during the Hundred Years' War between those two countries. She led the French army to victory at Orléans in 1429. A year later she was captured and given to the English, who turned her over to a French church court, which tried and convicted her for heresy because she believed she should obey her voices rather than church officials. She was burned at the stake in 1431. Twenty-five years later, she was retried and found innocent and, in 1920, the Church made her a saint.

A group of heretics being burned

Joan at the stake, from a 1484 manuscript

The Middle Ages 23

Life in the Middle Ages
Society and Culture

Mediaeval thought

Philosophical thought in ancient Greece was focused on reason, the investigation of nature and the search for human happiness. In the Middle Ages, thinkers were more interested in finding salvation after death through religion. In the fourth century, the Christian philosopher St. Augustine stated that the Christian emphasis on faith and emotion and the Greek insistence on reason are interrelated and that man needs both. Following his death, there were not many contributions to Western philosophy for the next few centuries.

During the twelfth century, the works of Aristotle, Plato and other Greek philosophers were translated by Arab scholars and came to the attention of theologians in Western Europe. The Spanish jurist and physician Averroës, who was the most important Muslim philosopher of his time, studied the works of Aristotle and his analysis had a profound effect on Christian philosophers.

Mediaeval thought is closely tied to the Christian Church. The Church was primarily responsible for preserving the work and writings of Greek philosophers like Plato and Aristotle, and since few people outside the clergy had any learning, mediaeval philosophers were also men of the Church.

St. Thomas Aquinas was the greatest intellectual of the mediaeval period. He was able to reconcile St. Augustine's theology with Aristotle's insistence on reason. He accepted God's existence on the basis of faith, but offered five rational proofs of His existence to support his belief. His doctrine became the accepted philosophy of the Roman Catholic church, and continued to influence philosophers into the twentieth century.

St. Thomas Aquinas (1225-74), born of an aristocratic Italian family, became a Dominican monk while still a student at the University of Naples.

The development of universities

Mediaeval universities originated in places where students gathered to hear learned teachers lecture about their particular subject. By the twelfth century, the University of Paris was the centre for theology and philosophy and the University of Bologna was the centre for law. By the thirteenth century, Oxford and Cambridge were established in England, and by the fourteenth, universities existed in Heidelberg and Prague. By the fifteenth century, universities had proliferated all over Western Europe.

Beyond the professional disciplines, the universities also taught the liberal arts. In the mediaeval curriculum, there were seven liberal arts grouped into two divisions, called the trivium and the quadrivium. The three "rhetorical arts" — grammar, logic and rhetoric — made up the trivium, and the quadrivium was composed of the more specialized arts: arithmetic, geometry, astronomy and music. Music was categorized with the sciences because the Greeks, in particular the philosopher and mathematician Pythagoras, had developed an elaborate scientific rationale for it, including the ratio of the vibrations that produced the different notes and their relationship to each other.

Students listening to a lecture at the University of Paris

Life in the Middle Ages

Science

The team in the background is pulling the plow. The pair in front is pulling a harrow to smooth out the furrows.

Invention timeline

500   Arabic numerals (1, 2, 3) began to replace Roman numerals (I, II, III).

600   Plows were invented in Mesopotamia about 3500 BC, but the simple plow was not effective against the heavy soils in Europe. When the mouldboard plow, with its curved blade that turns over the earth, was developed by Germanic farmers, farming became much more efficient.

868   The oldest printed book is a scroll printed in China using carved wooden blocks.

900   During the tenth century, the crossbow made its appearance. It was made of a metal bow fixed to a wooden stock, and it could shoot an arrow 300 metres or 1 000 feet.

1000   The spinning wheel was invented in India in the early eleventh century, but did not make its way to Europe until the early fourteenth century.

1065   Exactly when stained glass began to appear in church windows is unclear but the oldest surviving stained glass windows date from 1065. They are in the Augsburg Cathedral in Germany.

1090   The magnetic compass that floats in water was invented in China.

1180   Rudders began to be used on Arab ships and can be seen in pictures of the Crusades at the end of the 1100s.

A spinning wheel

An early stained glass window

A compass

You can see the steersman in control of the rudder at the stern of the ship on the left.

The Middle Ages

Science

Life in the Middle Ages

Invention timeline

1200   The Bishop of Lincoln, England, suggested using glass lenses to magnify things.

1250   The longbow was invented in Wales. As tall as the archer himself, the longbow was faster to load and fire than the crossbow.

1280   The Chinese learned how to use gunpowder to fire cannon.

1286   Venetian glassmakers ground lenses to use as reading glasses.

1300   The first accurate mechanical clocks came into use in the fourteenth century. When they began to be installed in church towers where everyone could see them, people began to use them to organize their daily life.

1300   Lacemaking began in Flanders early in the century. Lace was used as a decoration on clothing for both men and women.

1350   Guns like miniature cannons were being used in Europe. They were so long that soldiers using them had to prop up the muzzle end on something so they could shoot. By the fourteenth century, artillery had completely changed the face of warfare.

A magnifying glass

Early eyeglasses

The Middle Ages   27

The Arts in the Middle Ages — Literature

Early English literature

Old English poetry was primarily designed to be chanted. Since very few people could read and write, the Anglo-Saxon bards would repeat the sacred legends that were part of the tribal culture. The first work to be written down was the epic poem *Beowulf*, composed in the eighth century. It told the story of the hero Beowulf who destroyed the monster Grendel, Grendel's mother and a fire-breathing dragon. After the Norman Conquest, French became the language of the nobility and literature, and Latin was still the language used for learned works. It was not until the fourteenth century that English was used again by the ruling classes. Around 1390, Geoffrey Chaucer, a soldier and a public servant, wrote *The Canterbury Tales*, the first important work in English literature. Chaucer used the framework of a pilgrimage to the shrine at Canterbury to portray people from all levels of English society with a humour that is sometimes gentle and sometimes cutting. Rather later than Chaucer but still within the mediaeval tradition is Sir Thomas Malory's *La Mort d'Arthur* (1469-70), a collection of stories about King Arthur and the Knights of the Round Table, especially about the love of Sir Lancelot for Queen Guinevere.

Early French literature

The earliest written works in French were the *chansons de geste*, long poems about the exploits of Christian knights. Poet-musicians called *troubadours* in the language of southern France and *trouvères* in the north were the first in France to write in the native language. One group of *chansons* dealt with the knights who served the Church. The hero was Charlemagne, who is portrayed as saving Christianity. Most famous is the *Chanson de Roland*, written at the end of the eleventh century, about the heroic deeds of Roland, a knight at Charlemagne's court. Other *chansons* were based on Celtic folktales. One of the most important poets of these chansons was Chrétien de Troyes, who wrote poems about chivalry and courtly love based on the legends surrounding the English King Arthur and his knights. Popular in the twelfth and thirteenth centuries were the *fabliaux*, short, earthy tales satirizing human failings and flouting authority. At about the same time, the 22 000-line *Roman de la Rose* was written, describing love as a rosebud, living in a garden that symbolized the life of chivalry. One of the best-known mediaeval poets in France was François Villon, who lived from about 1431 to 1463. He was a scholar and a petty criminal and he wrote with a zest for life that was combined with his era's concern for sin and the imminence of death.

A portrait of Chaucer as a pilgrim from a 12th century manuscript

This illustration for the *Chanson de Roland* portrays the death of Roland's lady, the beautiful Aude, in the arms of King Charlemagne.

This picture from the *Livre de Messire Lancelot du Lac* shows the knights of the Round Table amazed by the appearance of the Holy Grail, the relic that was the object of their quest.

Early German literature

The oldest known piece of literature written in German is an epic poem called *Hildebrandslied*, about the battle between the hero Hildebrand and his son. It was written about 800 and only fragments survive. Then for the next couple of centuries, most literary works were written in Latin, with an oral tradition in German consisting of songs and ballads sung at the royal courts. Epic poetry was written during the twelfth and thirteenth century, often modelled on the *chansons de geste*, but expressing German ideals. The most famous is the *Nibelungenlied*, upon which the nineteenth century composer Richard Wagner based his opera-cycle, *The Ring of the Nibelungen*. There were also epics in which an animal was the hero, like *Reinecke Fuchs* (Reynard the Fox). The German counterpart to the French troubadours and trouvères were the minnesingers, whose poetry, generally set to music, not only told of love, but also dealt with religion and politics.

Italian literature

One of the greatest Italian writers was also one of the first. Dante Alighieri (1265-1321) is the author of *La divina commedia* (*The Divine Comedy*), an epic poem that is one of the masterpieces of all time. The poem is divided into three sections, entitled *Inferno* (*Hell*), *Purgatorio* (*Purgatory*) and *Paradiso* (*Paradise*), and it describes the poet's journey beyond the grave under the guidance of the ancient Roman poet Virgil and the poet's love, Beatrice. It is a dramatization of mediaeval Christian theology, philosophy, politics and science. It is also a morality tale about how reason and love can purify man's soul and bring him peace.

In this portrait, Dante Alighieri is pictured against a background of the three regions he explores on his voyage.

The other poet who was important in the development of Italian as a literary language was Petrarch (1304-74). He is seen as the first modern poet. In his *Canzoniere*, consisting of 317 poems written to his beloved, Laura, he perfected the sonnet form and inspired other poets like Chaucer and Shakespeare. The third important Italian writer of the period is Giovanni Boccaccio (1313-75). His masterpiece is *Il Decamerone* (*The Decameron*), a collection of 100 stories that alternate between wit and tragedy in dealing with the urban society of his time.

The Arts in the Middle Ages   Literature

Theatre

Mediaeval theatre began in the churches with liturgical drama, scenes from the Bible that were designed to teach religious lessons, spoken in Latin. As the plays began to have more secular content, they moved outside the churches and were spoken in the local language. These plays are called miracle or mystery plays. They were generally performed in the town market places on religious feast days, like Easter or other holy days, and especially came to be connected with the Feast of Corpus Christi. Each play was a cycle of as many as forty scenes and produced by everyone in the community. Each trade guild would be responsible for a scene, so the boatbuilders might do Noah's Ark, for example, or the fishmongers Jonah and the Whale. In England, people built pageant cars with the stage sets built on them, rather like modern-day parade floats, that would be moved to different places in the town. In France, people tended to build sets side-by-side on a long stage in front of the audience, who would move from scene to scene.

A scene from *The Torture of St. Apollonia*

The director in the middle holds the script and a baton, rather like a conductor.

In the 1400s, the morality play emerged. These differed from the mystery plays in that they did not present scenes from the Bible, and they were usually performed by professional minstrels, not the townspeople. One of the best known English morality plays is *Everyman*, in which characters like Gluttony, Fellowship, Good Deeds and Knowledge accompany Everyman on his journey through life, as he learns that only Good Deeds and Knowledge will lead him to salvation.

This platform stage was typical of French mystery plays. The set-like structures are placed in a row, moving from heaven on the left to the mouth of hell on the right.

Architecture

Romanesque architecture

From its headquarters in Rome, the Church spread what was left of Roman tradition and culture throughout the mediaeval world. Most of the major architectural works were built for the Church, and the first architects in the Middle Ages were monks, so it was natural that elements of Roman style and technology were the starting point for mediaeval architecture. The style, which flourished from 1000 to about 1250 or a bit later, was called Romanesque.

The major achievement of Romanesque architects was the development of stone-vaulted buildings. Before this, roofs were made of wood, which was easily destroyed by fire. Used for ceilings or roofs, vaults are arch-like structures that are held together by the pressure of the stones that make up the arch. They require very heavy walls and piers to support their weight, so Romanesque buildings are massive.

Mediaeval churches generally had an impressive façade on the wall that housed the main entrance. There were often towers on either side and a great deal of sculptural detail and carving on the surface. Stained glass windows were used in many locations around the church to tell religious stories. Because the windows were usually long and narrow, they usually depicted standing figures from the Bible. The colour came from adding various metallic substances to the melted glass, and the artist painted on details like facial features and lines in the clothing. Brilliant blue, red, yellow and green were the predominant colours, with pinkish shades for skin tones.

St-Savin-sur-Gartempe, France (1060-1115)

The barrel-vaulted roof is supported by rows of pillars.

The Abbey church, Vézelay, shows a similar construction with windows in the second story.

The west façade, Notre-Dame-la-Grande, Poitiers, France, early twelfth century

The stone-carved relief shows figures in wall arcades, sitting and standing. The scales on the turrets are supposed to look like Roman tile.

The Arts in the Middle Ages — Architecture

Gothic architecture

Gothic architecture began in France around 1140, and spread across Europe from there. The most important buildings were done for the Church. It began with the development of the ribbed vault early in the century. Thin stone arches rested on pillars and met each other in pointed arches, with the spaces in between filled with smaller stones. This created a vault that was lighter and thinner. Stone roofs are still very heavy, though, and in order to counteract the pressure pushing the wall outwards, builders used huge piles of stone or buttresses on the outside wall pushing against this force. They also developed a new kind of buttress called a flying buttress, which was connected by an arch to the point at which the rib begins to spring. The flying buttresses transferred the outward push to a downward one, stabilizing the whole structure. These two developments meant that walls could now be made much thinner and have more area devoted to windows, and the interior of the church could be much taller. Gothic churches are more delicate-looking than the Romanesque, and inside, with the increased number of stained-glass windows, the sense of space, the verticals from the ribs and the pointed arches, everything seems focussed heavenward.

With more space for glass, stained glass artists developed rose windows. These were huge round windows whose divisions looked like the petals on a rose. Rose windows, which often depicted stories about the Virgin Mary, the Mother of Christ, were placed in the west end of the church and on the walls of the transepts, the crossways aisle. As well, the subjects of the other windows in Gothic churches became more varied, portraying the life of Christ, the lives of the Saints, or the Last Judgement, even showing more secular subjects like the different work done in the course of a year as the seasons change. New colours became available, like deep purples and dark greens.

The nave in the Cathedral in Durham, England, showing the first ribbed vaulting (1093-1130)

The west façade of the Cathedral of Notre-Dame in Paris, which was built between 1200 and 1250

The interior of Notre-Dame

North rose window, Chartres

32 The Middle Ages

Secular architecture

Castles were fortresses built by kings or lords to defend their territory. The earliest ones were just wooden buildings on mounds of earth, or mottes, surrounded by a ditch. Later they often added a wall some distance away from the fortification, and the ground between was called the bailey. This kind of fortress is known as a motte-and-bailey castle, and it was the most common kind of structure by the eleventh century. The Normans were particularly good at building and defending them. The next development was adding a tall stone keep or donjon inside the bailey, with thick walls and small windows. The ditches became moats, preferably filled with water. Access to the castle was over a drawbridge that could be raised by the forces inside. The keep was the strongest part of the castle and the place where everyone retired when the outer defences had given way. It contained a well, the lord's private apartments, usually on the second floor for greater security, and everything necessary to sustain a long siege. In the stone walls of the castle and the outer fortifications were narrow holes though which soldiers could shoot arrows, or drop missiles on the enemy. Other types of castles were built on other types of terrain, but the principle was the same: to occupy a position higher than your enemy so you could see him coming and aim down on him from above.

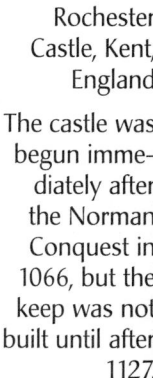

Rochester Castle, Kent, England

The castle was begun immediately after the Norman Conquest in 1066, but the keep was not built until after 1127.

The Duke of Orleans imprisoned in the Tower of London, after his capture with other French nobles at the Battle of Agincourt during the Hundred Years' War

The residences of the lower nobility were considerably less grand and generally only fortified to the extent that was necessary for the level of peace in the area. The manor house was the centre of village life apart from the church, and its great hall was used for gathering everyone together for feasts and celebrations. Inside the defensive wall would be found the great hall, the kitchens, the chapel, and various farm buildings like stables and barns. There might well be a moat.

This moated stone manor house dates from the thirteenth century, but the original wooden buildings were replaced with stone 200 years later.

These openings allowed archers to shoot down at their enemies while remaining protected.

The Arts in the Middle Ages

Painting and Decorative Arts

The early Middle Ages

Frescos, or wall paintings, were common from the time of Charlemagne. We know that frescos telling the lives of the saints and illustrating the Bible were painted on church walls during the early Middle Ages, but unfortunately very few survive. It is thought that the style may have been similar to that found in the illuminated manuscripts of the time.

Manuscripts were not merely copied, they were embellished with paintings and illustrations. Monks made pigments for painting from powdered earth substances, metal ores, and plants, which they were able to paint on the paper by mixing them with liquefied beaten egg whites so they would flow off a brush. Gold leaf was made by hammering gold into sheets as thin as a single layer of Kleenex. The earliest illuminations were done in the seventh century at Celtic monasteries in England and Ireland. Other styles developed in different regions and monastic schools over the next 500 years.

The beginning of the Gospel of Saint Matthew, from the Lindisfarne Gospels, early seventh century, is typical of the Celtic school, in which interwoven, abstract, geometric designs illuminate initial letters, borders, and sometimes whole pages.

This illuminated capital from the Book of Jeremiah is from the twelfth century Winchester Bible. The capital letter is illustrated with a biblical scene.

34   The Middle Ages

Painting and Decorative Arts | The Arts in the Middle Ages

The early Middle Ages

Metalwork was a well-developed art form in the early Middle Ages, and much of it was for church ritual, chalices to hold the wine and candlesticks for the altar, for example. Other important works were reliquaries, the receptacles built to hold the relics of saints. Relics were part of a deceased saint's body or belongings, which were often believed to have the power to make miracles, and were thus the objects of pilgrimages.

The most important work of textile art from the earlier Middle Ages is the Bayeux Tapestry. It is an embroidered illustration of the conquest of England by William the Conqueror. The events of the Norman conquest are recorded in more detail in the tapestry than in contemporary written accounts, and it is a wonderful source of information about life at the time.

The reliquary of St. Foy, in Conques, France. St. Foy was a little girl in the time of the Roman Empire who refused to worship idols and so was martyred. Various miracles, curing blindness, for example, were credited to her relics, so the faithful built a church in her honour and provided this figure to contain them.

This panel of the Bayeux Tapestry illustrates the death of Edward II of England. In the upper part, he is shown handing over his power to Harold, and in the lower one, he is wrapped in his shroud. The Latin inscription says, *"Et hic defunctus est* [and here he is dead]."

The Middle Ages 35

The Arts in the Middle Ages — Painting and Decorative Arts

The later Middle Ages

Duccio, *Madonna Enthroned*, 1308-11

More mediaeval paintings remain from the later Middle Ages, so it is possible to get a clearer idea of the style then. The figures are stylized and two-dimensional, and the artists used bright colours and lots of gold.

In the late 1300s, influenced by the pre-Renaissance artists in Italy, Gothic painting began to have a different sense of space, and seems less two-dimensional. One of the great art patrons of the period, other than the Church, was Jean de France, the Duke of Berry, and one book remains to us from his patronage of two manuscript artists, the Limbourg Brothers—*Les Très Riches Heures du duc de Berry (The Very Rich Hours of the Duke of Berry)*. The pictures that illustrate this Book of Hours, a small book with prayers for all the hours in the religious day, give us a rich picture of life in the French countryside and at court as well.

The Limbourg Brothers, October from the *Très Riches Heures*, 1413-16

The Limbourg Brothers, January from *Les Très Riches Heures*

36 The Middle Ages

Painting and Decorative Arts

The Arts in the Middle Ages

The later Middle Ages

With the work of Giotto, a fourteenth-century Italian painter, painting took a new turn. Giotto rejected the traditional flat, two-dimensional style for rounder, more sculptural human figures. He also preferred more muted shades than the typical bright colours of the mediaeval period. Giotto's works were entirely religious, and some of his frescos still remain. Particularly important is the fresco series illustrating the lives of the Virgin and Christ in the Arena Chapel, Padua.

The painter Jan van Eyck, from Flanders, bridges the gap between mediaeval art and that of the Renaissance. His works are much more naturalistic and his portraits express genuine personality. He also developed the technique of working with oil paints, which had been known for a hundred years, but hardly used. This gave him a more varied colour range and more dramatic lights and darks.

Giotto, *The Lamentation of Christ*, 1305-6

Giotto, *Madonna Enthroned*, c. 1310

Jan van Eyck, *Arnolfini and his Wife*, 1434

Jan van Eyck, *Madonna* (detail), 1426-27
Notice how van Eyck's Madonna looks so much more like a real person.

The Middle Ages

The Arts in the Middle Ages — Sculpture

Romanesque sculpture

Most Romanesque sculpture was incorporated into church architecture, and it often served a structural function as well as artistic one. The artists of the time liked to decorate with scenes from the Bible and animals, both real and imaginary. Often the creatures are quite fantastic.

Other sculptural works on a smaller scale were done as well. Sculptors carved in ivory and worked with gold, using the same pictorial styles that are found in larger works.

This sculpture decorates a column in the Cathedral of Saint-Lazare in Autun, France, 1125-35. It shows Mary and the baby Jesus escaping from King Herod on a donkey led by Joseph.

A candlestick made for Gloucester Cathedral, England

Carving in ivory showing a priest leading a service

The main door at the Abbey Church, Vézelay, France, 12th century

The relief shows Christ surrounded by his apostles; the people all over the world who will listen to their preaching are portrayed in the panels surrounding the main carving and include some very strange creatures, like men with wolves' heads.

38 The Middle Ages

Sculpture

The Arts in the Middle Ages

Gothic sculpture

In the later Middle Ages, churches continued to be decorated with sculpted scenes and figures, and sculpture was still primarily architectural in nature. Often very large statue-columns were placed on either side of the doors on the highly decorated west fronts of the cathedrals. The earliest of these, dating from about 1150, are found in Chartres Cathedral in France, and in the 100 years or so that it took to construct the cathedral, it is possible to see a change from the stiff, linear Romanesque style to a more naturalistic, rounded figure, standing out more from the column behind it. When these sculptures are compared to those at Rheims Cathedral, which was begun about the time Chartres was finished, one can see that here the new Gothic style is fully developed.

The Bamberg rider is the first European example of a freestanding statue since the time of the Romans. Attached to a pier in the cathedral in Bamberg, Germany, it was made about 1240.

Virgin and Child in ivory

The new naturalism was seen in smaller sculptural works as well.

The west portal of Chartres Cathedral, late 12th century

The statue-columns from the west portal of Chartres carved in approximately 1150 are still in the Romanesque style.

These statue-columns around the south transept door at Chartres were done about 60 years later, and they show how the style was beginning to change.

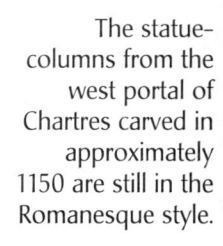

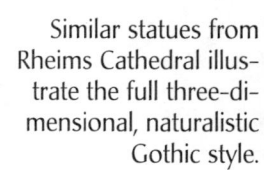

Similar statues from Rheims Cathedral illustrate the full three-dimensional, naturalistic Gothic style.

The Middle Ages   39

Musical Life in the Middle Ages   **The Church**

Cathedrals

Most musicians in the Middle Ages worked for the Church. It was in fact the main employer of artists in all fields, from the builders of the great cathedrals to the stonemasons who did the carvings to the people who wrote and sang the music for its services.

The cathedral was the most important place of worship in any diocese, and the seat of the bishop. In a way, the cathedral was the bishop's court and it had to be magnificent. There was a great need for music to enhance church services and attest to the glory of God so that the congregation, from royalty down to the ordinary peasant, would be impressed by the splendour of Christianity and its earthly manifestation in the Catholic Church. In addition to the daily mass, there were special services for special days in the church calendar, like Christmas and Easter and other feast days, and music was required for the texts that were particular to that day. Most church musicians were in holy orders. They would compose the needed chants, sing in the choir, and perhaps serve as music director for the cathedral. Most musicians got their training as choirboys. Cathedrals had choir schools attached to them, and they had competitions to attract young choristers. The boys learned how to sing and play an instrument, and were able to find work as church or court musicians when they left school.

The cathedral of Milan, begun in 1386

Pisa Cathedral, 1053–1272

No one attending a service in this cathedral could fail to be impressed by the splendour of the Church.

40   **The Middle Ages**

The Church | Musical Life in the Middle Ages

Monasteries

Music also played an important role in the monasteries. Life in a monastery was organized around its services. Monks and nuns spent a good deal of their day in prayer. Every day there was a mass, of course, but there were also eight other services that took place from two or three in the morning until early evening. These services were largely sung, so a large number of chants were required. Monks would compose new music and make small changes to traditional melodies. Music was seen as an act of prayer; it enlarged the devotional experience. There were no congregations to impress in the monasteries and the music was not intended to gratify an audience, but to please God.

Monks were often music scholars and there was much debate about the philosophical and theoretical aspects of music. Many of the dissertations on music theory written in the Middle Ages were by monks.

This manuscript illustration shows a group of monks in their choir stalls chanting the text for one of the many services that took place in the religious day.

A group of monks reading the music from a manuscript

Monks singing

Musical Life in the Middle Ages

The Court

Musicians, poets and minstrels

There was, of course, music outside the churches. There was a continual struggle for power between the Church and the nobility, and the kings and barons used music as a way of increasing the prestige of their courts. Gradually, as the nobility's influence grew, the Church lost its position as the only sponsor of the arts. The courts developed their own musical culture based on secular songs that reflected the lives lived there. Certain aristocrats in particular had reputations as patrons of the arts, like Eleanor of Aquitaine, who was married to King Louis VII of France and later to Henry II of England, and was one of the most powerful women of the Middle Ages.

The court poet-composers—called troubadours in the south of France, trouvères in the north, and minnesingers in German-speaking regions—were the most important composers of secular music. The words troubadour and trouvère mean "finder," or in musical terms, composer. Many of them were aristocrats themselves, like Guillaume IX of Aquitaine, and Richard I of England, called Richard the Lion-Heart. The troubadours flourished in twelfth- and thirteenth-century Provence, and the tradition moved into the courts of northern France when Eleanor of Aquitaine married Louis VII and brought her southern traditions to the court in Paris. Their works, which established the form for secular songs for several centuries, were strongly influenced by chivalry and the ideal of courtly love. It is known that there were women troubadours, but all the known trouvères were men.

A troubadour entertains two ladies while accompanying himself on a vielle, a mediaeval fiddle.

A woman troubadour, the Countess of Die

In the south of France, women too wrote songs about courtly love.

42 The Middle Ages

The Court

Musical Life in the Middle Ages

Musicians, poets and minstrels

Musicians were also hired to entertain the courts. Music was needed as an accompaniment for dining, dancing and tournaments and to enhance court ceremonies, civic processions and military campaigns. Instrumental music was much more prominent in secular music than in the church, where it was distrusted as likely to inflame the passions rather than promote worship.

At the bottom end of the social scale were the minstrels, or jongleurs, men and women who wandered from town to town. They sang and played instruments, juggled, did tricks and animal acts, and generally entertained the artisans and peasants. Sometimes they performed the well-known troubadour songs, other times they wrote their own, often weaving into them the news and gossip of the day, an important function in a time when newspapers did not exist.

A pair of minstrels, a juggler and a flute player

A wandering minstrel playing a lute

The Middle Ages

Characteristics of Music in the Middle Ages

General Features

The development of notation

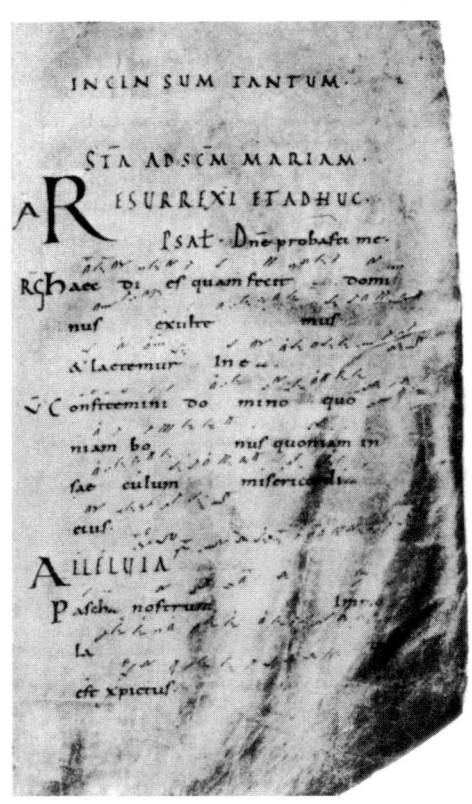

The earliest mediaeval music was monophonic, meaning it had only one line of melody. It was handed down from generation to generation. But as the amount of music grew, musicians needed a written reminder of the melodies for particular plainsong chants, and a system of notation began to evolve. Early plainsong notation was very simple, little signs called neumes that suggested whether the voice should rise or fall. There was no staff with lines to indicate the pitches; the neumes were just written in above the words. In reality, the neumes were a sort of crib sheet, used to remind the singers of the melody for chants they had already committed to memory. This system continued to develop with horizontal lines, one coloured red to indicate the note F and another yellow to indicate C.

In the eleventh century, Guido of Arezzo, a Benedictine monk in Avellana, Italy, further refined the system by adding a black line above F and another above the C, to make a grid of four lines so that all the pitches fell either on a line or in a space. It then became possible to establish the relationship of one pitch to another.

Guido also invented solmisation, a system of designating the notes of the scale with syllables, which is the basis for the modern system of sol-fa, or sight singing. The first six lines of the chant celebrating John the Baptist each begin with a higher note than the preceding line, so Guido named the notes for the first syllable of each line:

Ut queant laxis / **Re**sonare fibris / **Mi**ra gestorum
Famuli tuorum / **Sol**ve pollute / **La**bi reatum

The same syllables are used today with the addition of the seventh note. The seventh or leading note was included in the scale at a later time and its name, si, was chosen because the seventh line in the chant begins *Sanctus Iohannes*, the Latin for Saint John. Nowadays do is used instead of ut in most languages, and si has become ti.

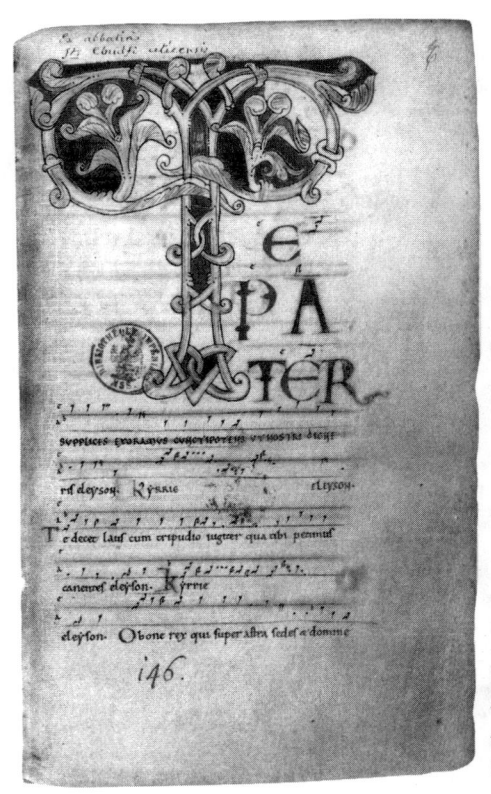

This manuscript, c. 900, is the earliest surviving manuscript showing the system of squiggly lines and dots called neumes that were written in over the words as a memory aid to the singers.

This manuscript shows the horizontal lines used to indicate pitch.

44 Music in the Middle Ages

General Features

Characteristics of Music in the Middle Ages

The development of notation

In the twelfth century, the curved lines of the neumes changed, and the separate notes within them were indicated by broad horizontal lines, diamond-shaped dots and very thin vertical lines, called ligatures. This produced rather squared-off notes, sometimes with tails added, that resemble our modern notation. By the thirteenth century, the time values for the different shapes were set down. The note with the longest duration, the longa (¶), could be divided into two or three breves (■), which in turn could be divided into two or three semibreves (♦), which could further be divided into minims (♩). This system lasted until the sixteenth century, when notes became rounded.

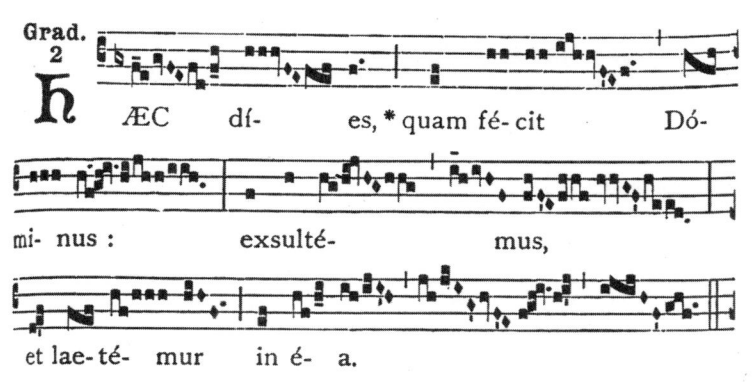

The opening of the Haec dies showing ligatures on a staff

To coordinate and synchronize two or more voices, the composer had to be able to indicate not only pitch but also rhythm for each of the voices. The later development of polyphonic music, or music with two or more melodic lines, would never have been possible without this complex system of notation.

Beautifully illuminated manuscripts like this one were not for everyday use. They were generally made as munificent gifts for royalty or princes of the Church.

This eleventh-century manuscript is a collection of music entitled the *Recueil de ballades, motets et chansons*. The shape reflects the subject matter of the songs.

Music in the Middle Ages

Characteristics of Music in the Middle Ages — Specific Features

Plainsong

The early music of the Christian Church grew in part out of the monophonic music from ancient Greek, Hebrew and Syrian cultures. Called plainsong or plainchant, it is vocal music, written for the choirs found at all cathedrals, monasteries and abbeys. Plainsong is also called Gregorian chant after Gregory I, who was Pope from 590 to 604. He decided that all existing music should be gathered together into a uniform liturgy throughout the church. A great deal of plainsong is left to us, about 3 000 chants, each one with a particular meaning in the liturgy.

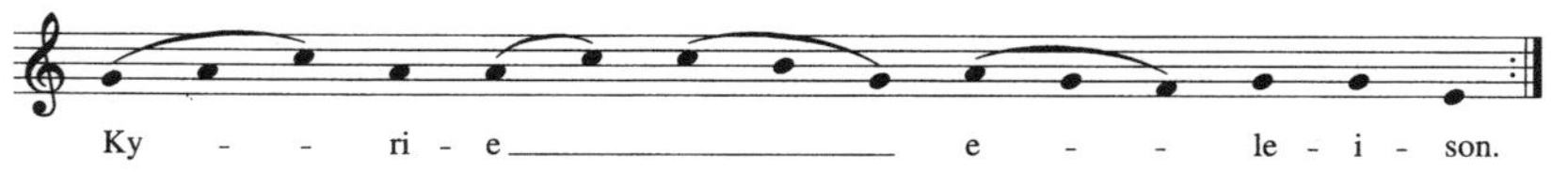

In pa-ra-di-sum de-du-cant
An example of syllabic chant

Plainsong has only one line of melody, but that line can be varied in a number of different ways. It can be sung by one person, or by a whole choir, or it may alternate between the two. There are several different genres with different melodic styles, varying from near monotone to songs with hundreds of notes ranging more than an octave. Some chants have only one note for each syllable in the text—these are called syllabic chants. Melismatic chants have many notes attached to a single syllable. The style of the chant depended on its role in the service. Psalms were usually chanted with only a slight variation in pitch, but the most important parts of the mass were embellished with intricate melodies.

Ky - ri - e   e - le - i - son.
An example of melismatic chant

Plainsong is very recognizable for its tranquil, celestial stream of sound, free from a regular beat or accent. It moves along in a meandering line, sometimes following the rhythm of the text, breaking into phrases rather like the spoken word. Another factor contributing to the sound of plainsong is that the notes are based on pitches organized into modes, which mediaeval musicians gradually derived from the Greek theories of music. Each mode sounds subtly different, but the shadings of sound are very gentle. Because there is only one melodic line, it is easy to follow the direction of the music and be carried along with its flow.

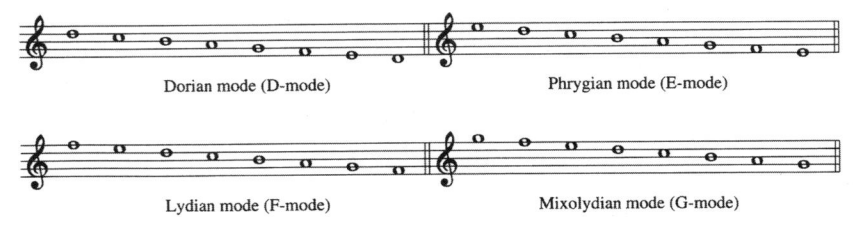

Pope Gregory I

Dorian mode (D-mode)   Phrygian mode (E-mode)
Lydian mode (F-mode)   Mixolydian mode (G-mode)

The main modes, whose names come from the Greek, are organized around four different starting pitches: D, E, F and G. Each mode corresponds approximately to playing the white keys on the piano from these four starting points. Their different sound qualities come from the particular intervals that occur in that mode, the pattern of whole tones and semitones that make up the scale.

Music in the Middle Ages

Specific features

Characteristics of Music in the Middle Ages

The mass

The form of the church service was relatively stable in Western Europe by the eleventh century. The central part of the mass is the communion, the ritual re-enactment of the Last Supper, designed to inspire the faithful with the certainty of life everlasting. Most people in the Middle Ages would not have understood the Latin text of the mass except by familiarity of use. In the most solemn service, the high mass, most of the prayers would be sung; in less formal services, they might merely be read aloud by the priest. Some parts of the mass, those which form the Ordinary, used the same words every time. Other parts, called the Proper, changed text depending on the feasts of the Church calendar that were being celebrated. There would be plainsong chants for each section of the liturgy, with spoken words intervening.

The Mass of St. Gilles

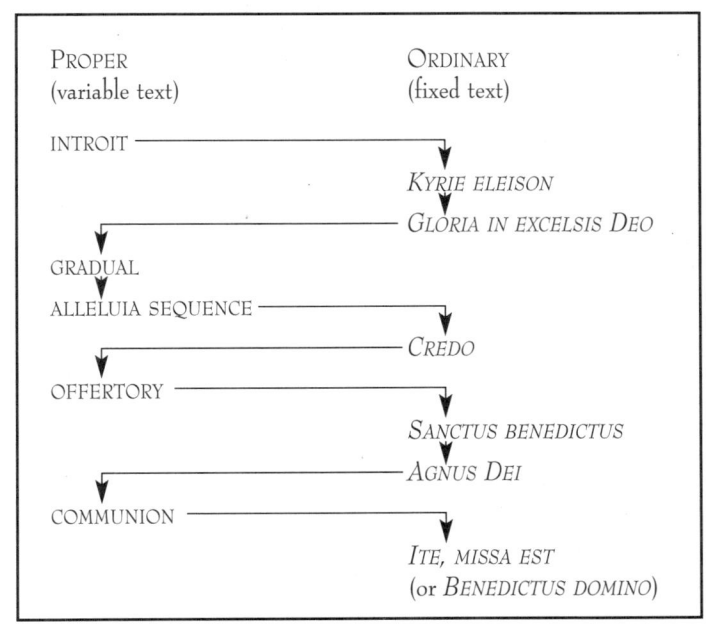

Ivory carving depicting monks celebrating the mass

STRUCTURE OF THE MASS

PROPER (variable text)	ORDINARY (fixed text)
INTROIT	
	KYRIE ELEISON
	GLORIA IN EXCELSIS DEO
GRADUAL	
ALLELUIA SEQUENCE	
	CREDO
OFFERTORY	
	SANCTUS BENEDICTUS
	AGNUS DEI
COMMUNION	
	ITE, MISSA EST (or BENEDICTUS DOMINO)

Music in the Middle Ages 47

Characteristics of Music in the Middle Ages — Specific Features

Secular song

The songs of the troubadours, trouvères and minnesingers were written in the vernacular, that is, their own language rather than the Latin of the Church. The troubadours spoke Provençal, the trouvères the language of northern France that is the basis for modern French, and the minnesingers, German. Typically, they wrote lyrical love songs to the noble ladies of their courts, who were idealized as beautiful unattainable creatures to whom the troubadours addressed unrequited sentiments of passion, devotion and respect. They also wrote songs praising the Virgin Mary, celebrating marriages, mourning deaths, describing the crusades—songs portraying their lives, in fact.

The musical style of the troubadours was adopted by the trouvères and then by the minnesingers. Most of the songs were monophonic, and the musical forms were closely related to the poetic structure, with specific rhythms derived from the metric system of the verse forms. Most common was the ballad, which had an AAB structure, but the rondeau, a song for solo voice with a choral refrain, and the virelay, in which the first and last lines of each stanza were the same, were also popular. These were called "fixed forms." Some melodies were like plainsong chants of the syllabic type, others more dancelike. The troubadours and trouvères tended to favour the modes with a "major" sound and they were the first to use the seventh note of the scale, a sound the Church rejected as unharmonious. About 300 troubadour songs and 1 400 trouvères have come down to us.

This illumination shows Heinrich von Meissen, called "Frauenlob" or champion of ladies, surrounded by musicians playing mediaeval instruments.

Specific Features

Characteristics of Music in the Middle Ages

Polyphony

The tenth and eleventh centuries are marked by one of the most important developments in Western music, the evolution of polyphony. Up to that point, music had only had one melodic line, but now composers began to experiment with two.

The earliest form of polyphony is called organum. It consists of a second line of melody added to a plainsong chant, sung with the same words at the same time. At first, the two melodies ran parallel to one another at the same interval, the notes of the second part a fourth or fifth below the first, in the free-flowing rhythm of the chant. This was called parallel organum.

Later, the second melody became more independent, going up when the chant went down, and vice versa.

Next, the second voice began to sing several notes to each single chant note, and the chant notes were held for a long time, like drones. At this point, the chant voice became the lower one, and was called the *cantus firmus*, or underlying melody. It was also called the *tenor*, from the Latin *tenure*, meaning "to hold," the voice that holds the chant.

The next stage, which occurred around the end of the twelfth century, was to add a second melody, which had to fit with both the chant and the other melody. At roughly the same time, definite rhythms were introduced, and the different voices could each have a different rhythmic pattern. These new forms of organum were developed at the Cathedral of Notre-Dame in Paris under the leadership of the monk Léonin and his successor Pérotin. Pérotin wrote organa for as many as four voices at once.

Parallel organum

Organum showing contrary movement

Haec dies chant showing the long low notes or drones in the *cantus firmus*

A three-voice chant by Pérotin called *Alleluia Nativitas*

Music in the Middle Ages

Characteristics of Music in the Middle Ages — Specific Features

Polyphony

About the middle of the thirteenth century, musicians began writing a new kind of three-part work, called a motet, in which they added words for the upper voices to sing. (In French, *mot* means word.) The motet consisted of a piece of Gregorian chant in Latin, in which the composer kept the original pitches, but gave them a specific rhythm, usually making them very long notes. This part was the tenor, which was then set against one, two or three counter melodies. The middle voice, called the duplum, and the top voice, called the triplum, were set to completely different texts, and were rhythmically much more complex, often crossing over one another. Sometimes both voices would sing different texts in Latin, sometimes one would sing in Latin, the other in French. Often they combined sacred and secular texts in the upper voices of the same piece, while the tenor holds the structure together.

This illustrates a motet in which the triplum is in Latin and the duplum in French.

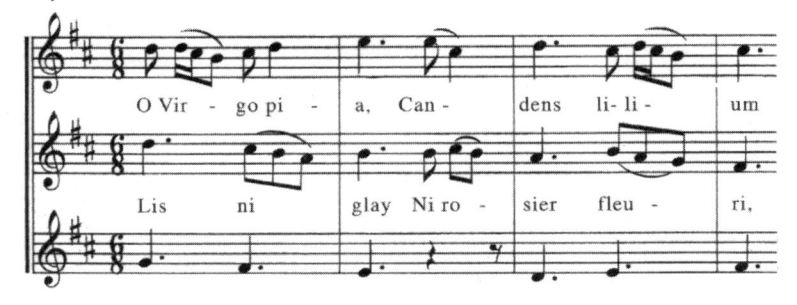

The first few bars of Machaut's *Hareu! Hareu! le feu / Helas! / Obediens*. The poem used by Guillaume de Machaut for the triplum tells of a lover who is being consumed by his love as though by fire. The different poem used for the duplum expresses the lover's despair in the face of his lady's coldness. The plainsong chant used for the tenor says "Obedient even unto death." It originally referred to Christ, but the sentiment fits very well within the context of courtly love.

Specific Features | **Characteristics of Music in the Middle Ages**

Ars nova

A new style of music arose in fourteenth-century France. It was called Ars nova, or new art, as opposed to Ars antiqua, the music of the previous few centuries. The term Ars nova came from the title of a work on the new style written in about 1320 by the composer Philippe de Vitry, one of its greatest proponents.

Music of the Ars nova was much more complex. Musicians were no longer bound by the rhythmic patterns used by the composers of the Ars antiqua. The development of mensural notation with notes of a specific duration gave them the ability to use duple metre instead of the triple metre that dominated the previous age. They also used different rhythms in the different voices. For the first time, composers treated the music for the mass as though the separate parts fitted together into an integrated whole. And they took a much greater interest in secular song. Polyphonic secular music in the form of the ballad, the virelay and the rondeau was an important part of fourteenth-century music. The most important composers of the Ars nova were Philippe de Vitry and Guillaume de Machaut.

A page from the *Roman de Fauvel* by Gervais de Bus

A manuscript of this poem made in 1316 incorporated 130 musical works of both the Ars antiqua and the Ars nova styles. Five pieces by Philippe de Vitry are included, allowing us to see some of the earliest examples of Ars nova music.

Music in the Middle Ages

Characteristics of Music in the Middle Ages

Specific Features

Instrumental music

Although vocal music still played a central role, by the 1300s instrumental music was increasingly popular. Instruments supported vocal music, either by accompanying singers or, most likely, by doubling their notes using a simple drone. Sometimes instrumental arrangements were made of vocal works, and of course instruments were essential for dance music. Instrumental music tended to be improvised and therefore was not often written down, but some written works remain to give us an idea of what it was like. The instruments themselves are often represented in paintings and books, and some early examples survive in museums.

Early instruments fall into the same general groupings as modern ones; there were strings, woodwinds, brass, percussion and keyboard instruments. They were divided according to whether they were soft (*bas*) or loud (*haut*). Instruments with a soft sound were generally used indoors and louder ones were used for outdoor entertainments. String instruments that were plucked, like the lute, the harp and the psaltery, or bowed, like the viele and the rebec, were used indoors, as were recorders and flutes. Outdoor instruments included the bagpipes, the shawm (an ancestor of the oboe), and the slide trumpet, which developed into the sackbut, a kind of early trombone. There were other instruments that were used indoors and out, like the crumhorn, a J-shaped woodwind with a double reed and a softer sound than the shawm, and the cornetto, a wooden horn with a mouthpiece like a brass instrument and finger holes like a woodwind. Drums included the large cylindrical tabors and small, bowl-shaped drums called nakers. Other percussion instruments were cymbals and bells. Organs were also used in the Middle Ages: large ones with no stops so that all the pipes sounded at once, requiring several men to pump the bellows, and smaller portative organs, with only one rank of pipes and a bellows the player could pump himself. Another popular instrument was the hurdy-gurdy, a kind of mechanized fiddle, with melody strings that are played through a keyboard and drone strings that sound when a wheel is turned.

a) string instruments
b) psaltery
c) horns
d) set of bells
e) flutes
f) bagpipes
g) hurdy-gurdies

Specific Features

Characteristics of Music in the Middle Ages

Dance music

There were a number of dance forms in the Middle Ages, many of them chain dances in which the dancers held hands and danced as a group. The carole was a ring dance perfomed as the dancers sang ballads. In the branle, the chain of dancers made a side-to-side movement by alternating large steps to the left and the same number of small steps to the right. The music was always in 4/4 time, but the speed varied. The farandole was also a chain dance, but the dancers followed the steps of a leader who wound through the streets of town accompanied by pipes and tabors playing in 6/8 time. The estampie was one of the first dances for couples, a slow stately dance accompanied by vieles. The music followed an aa, bb, cc form repeated up to seven times. Estampies are some of the earliest instrumental music that still exist. One of the most famous troubadour songs, "Kalenda Maya," was written to an existing estampie melody. The saltarello followed the estampie as an afterdance in the fourteenth century. It was a fast, leaping dance for couples in triple metre, either 3/4 or 9/8.

A group of aristocrats dancing a ring dance

Peasants doing a chain dance, accompanied by a bagpiper

An ivory box carved with dancing women

Lorenzetti, *The Roundelay of Young Women*

Music in the Middle Ages

Composers

Religious composers

Much liturgical music of the Middle Ages has come down to us marked Anonymous, but there are some composers whose names are known. One of the earliest was a woman, **Hildegard von Bingen (1098-1179)**, who was the prioress of the Benedictine monastery of Disibodenberg. Hildegard was given to the Church when she was quite young by her noble parents because she was their tenth child, a practice called tithing. She took her vows at the age of 15 and became Mother Superior of the order when she was 34. Something of a mystic, she experienced visions from the time she was a child. After the Church authenticated them, she recorded them in a book entitled *Scivias*. In 1147, she established a new Benedictine monastery in the Rhineland near Bingen and was involved in politics and diplomacy through her correspondence with popes, kings and archbishops. She wrote a large quantity of monophonic plainsongs, and a morality play called *Ordo virtutum*, or *The Play of the Virtues*, which depicts the battle between the Devil and the Virtues for the soul, Anima. Her *Symphonia armonia celestium revelationum* is a collection of 77 lyric poems, each with its own music.

An illumination from one of Hildegard von Bingen's manuscripts, showing her enveloped by the fire from heaven that came down to inspire her

There were two masters of music at the Cathedral of Notre-Dame in Paris in the twelfth century. The first was **Léonin (c. 1135-1201)** and the second, **Pérotin (c. 1160-1240)**. A large group of musicians were at the Cathedral, working under the leadership of Léonin, and his student Pérotin. Léonin is credited with developing organum, and he is believed to be the author of the *Magnus liber organi* (*The Great Book of Organum*), a collection of two-part organa for the whole church year. Léonin was also responsible for introducing definite rhythm patterns. Pérotin was the first to incorporate more than two voices, and he is known to have composed at least two four-part works. He also made additions to Léonin's *Magnus liber organi*.

54 Music in the Middle Ages

Troubadours and trouvères

We do at least know the names and a little bit about some of these poet-composers. One of the earliest troubadours was **Guillaume de Poitiers, the Duke of Aquitaine (1070-1127)** and Eleanor's grandfather. Another was a commoner named **Macabru**, who died around 1150. He was a foundling, raised by a rich man and apprenticed to a troubadour. **Bernart de Ventadour**, who lived in the second half of the twelfth century, was in service to Eleanor of Aquitaine before he retired to the abbey of Dalon. His work is thought to be the finest of all the Provençal poets. Eighteen of his complete musical compositions survive.

Well-known trouvères include **Richard the Lion-Heart (1157-99)**, son of Henry II of England and Eleanor of Aquitaine, probably better known as a crusader and for taking back the crown of England from his brother John, and **Adam de la Halle (c. 1237-87)**, a commoner. Adam was born in Arras, studied in Paris, and lived and travelled in Italy. His most famous work is *Le Jeu de Robin et Marion*, a secular drama about a knight's wooing of a shepherdess, which is regarded as a precursor of French comic opera. Many of his works survive, both monophonic and polyphonic.

Macabru depicted in an illumination

A page from Adam de la Halle's *Le Jeu de Robin et Marion*

Composers

Composers of Ars nova

Philippe de Vitry (1291-1361) was one of the most prominent promoters of the Ars nova, and the author of the music theory text from which the movement got its name. He was educated at the Sorbonne and rose to be a bishop. He was a clerk in the royal household in Paris and served Duke Jean of Normandy. In his treatise *Ars nova*, he explained the new theories of mensural notation, and introduced symbols for new note durations. He was important in the development of the motet. His surviving musical works are primarily secular motets in Latin on political subjects.

An illumination from the Roman de Fauvel by Machaut

Guillaume de Machaut (c. 1300-77) was perhaps the outstanding composer of the Ars nova, and his complete works are preserved in a series of illuminated manuscripts prepared for members of the French royalty. He was born near Rheims, took holy orders while still young, and then became secretary to John of Luxembourg, the King of Bohemia. He also served Charles, Duke of Normandy and King of France. As both a priest and a courtier, it is not surprising that he wrote both religious and secular music. All of his music has been preserved in 32 manuscripts and much of what we know about the music of his period comes from them. He is best known for his *Mass of Notre-Dame*, one of the earliest polyphonic mass settings. It was also one of the first to deal with the different sections of the mass as if they belonged to a unified whole. Most of Machaut's music is secular. Twenty-three motets survive, but he is also important for his monophonic lais and virelais, which preserve the tradition of the trouvères, and for his development of polyphonic ballads and rondeaus.

The beginning of Machaut's lai Le Remède de fortune

An illumination from Le Remède de fortune

56 Music in the Middle Ages

The Renaissance

The second half of this book presents the Renaissance.

The Piazza San Marco in Venice showing singers and instrumentalists taking part in a religious procession

The Renaissance came to Europe at different times depending on the region. It began in Italy in the fourteenth century, but did not reach some other parts of the continent until the sixteenth century. As a general guide, we talk about the Renaissance lasting from 1450 to 1600.

Renaissance means rebirth, and as such it is something of a misnomer. But the word was coined by nineteenth-century historians who saw this period as a rebirth of humanity after a long time of deterioration. Modern historians recognize that the period called the Renaissance was in many ways a continuation of the progress that had occurred during the Middle Ages. However, Renaissance intellectuals took much of their inspiration from ancient Greece and Rome. Their values were therefore more focused on human than on divine beings and their interests leaned more towards politics, language, literature and history than sacred issues.

| Life in the Renaissance | The Political Situation |

The Italian city states

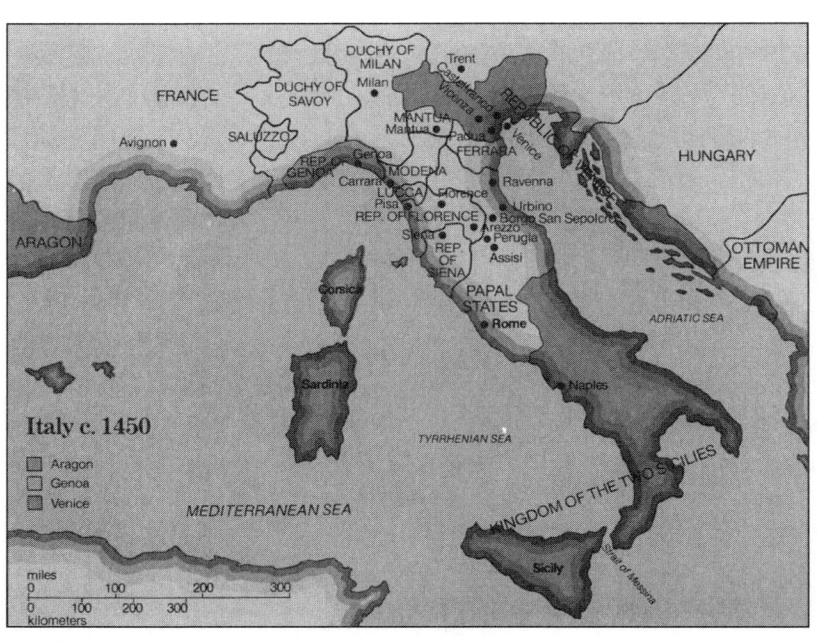

In Italy, feudalism never completely obliterated the urban centres of the old Roman empire. During the Middle Ages, the towns continued to grow and fight each other over territory, until the stronger ones took over the weaker ones and a system of regional power centres emerged. The population in each city was generally divided between warring factions, and the faction that was in power would banish the others. Trade and industry had made these cities powerful, but all the infighting was not good for business. The position of a chief magistrate therefore evolved, so that there would be someone to resolve the conflicts. Generally this position was held by a noble, and the people submitted to his rule for the sake of peace. So by the middle of the fifteenth century, northern Italy in particular was divided into city states that were governed by absolute rulers who tried to achieve their goals by diplomacy in the first instance, but who did not hesitate to go to war if diplomacy failed.

Often the position was hereditary. The most powerful and influential cities were Florence, Milan, Venice and Ferrara. Their wealth was responsible for growth in art, literature, science and thought that was the Renaissance.

Italy in 1490

Most of the independent city states were in the north. The land was more fertile and the area had better trade links with Europe. The Papal States, ruled by Rome, were in the middle. The Kingdom of Naples occupied most of the southern part of the peninsula.

The city of Florence
The famous dome on the cathedral overpowers the whole scene.

58 The Renaissance

The political Situation Life in the Renaissance

The Italian courts

Much of the cultural growth that occurred in the Italian Renaissance came as a result of the powerful families that ran the important city states. Patrons of the arts themselves, they also fostered a climate of support for the arts. Their cities were wealthy, and many of their citizens were well educated and more interested in the real world than the spiritual one. The conflict between the different states increased civic pride and their governments were willing to pay for beautiful buildings. They took an interest in town planning and the kind of artworks they commissioned were likely to be secular in nature.

Florence was dominated by the House of Medici, who were the pope's bankers. Cosimo de'Medici, who ruled from 1439 to 1464, was an important patron of writers and artists. He gave commissions to sculptors and architects, founded a library and supported scholars. His grandson, Lorenzo, called Lorenzo the Magnificent, made the Medici one of the most powerful families in Italy. He patronized Michelangelo and Botticelli, and encouraged patronage of the arts in others. The family produced two popes, Leo X and Clement VII, and two queens, Catherine, who married Henry II of France, and Marie, who married Henry IV of France.

In Milan, the ruling family was the Sforzas. They too maintained a splendid court and patronized the arts. Ludovico Sforza, who was Duke of Milan in the last half of the fifteenth century, employed Leonardo da Vinci to paint *The Last Supper* on the walls of the monastery Santa Maria delle Grazie. The Este family ruled the duchy of Ferrara, where their court was a centre of learning and the arts. The dukes of Urbino turned that city into a renowned art centre.

Cosimo de'Medici established the Medici as the dominant family in Florence.

Lorenzo de'Medici, known as the Magnificent, made the Medici one of the most powerful families in Italy.

Francesco Sforza, Duke of Milan

Leonello d'Este, Duke of Ferrara

The palace of the Duke of Urbino

A portrait of the Duke of Urbino, showing him reading one manuscript of his collection

The Renaissance

Life in the Renaissance — The Political Situation

The French monarchy

By the middle of the fifteenth century, the Valois kings of France had removed the English from their territory, ending the Hundred Years War. By the end of the century, they also had taken over the territory belonging to the Dukes of Burgundy in the east, and Brittany on the Atlantic coast, so that they reigned over the lands from the western seaboard to the Rhine River. Their attention then turned to Italy. In 1494, Charles VIII of France took an army into Italy to take the crown of the Kingdom of Naples. He won the battle but could not hold onto the territory and was forced to return home a year later. The kings of the early sixteenth century, Louis XII and Francis I, also lead armies into Italy to enforce France's claims to the Kingdom of Naples and the Duchy of Milan.

These wars did not gain France much territory, but they did enable the ideas and values of the Italian Renaissance to move over the Alps and into the rest of Europe. Francis in particular was fascinated with Italy and was responsible for the spread of many Renaissance ideas into France and the rest of Europe.

Francis I

Louis XII

This picture shows Francis I, on the white charger, and Charles V, the Holy Roman Emperor, behind him on the right, entering Paris in a royal procession.

60   The Renaissance

The Political Situation

Life in the Renaissance

The Spanish monarchy

With the marriage of Isabella of Castile and Ferdinand of Aragon in 1469, the two Spanish kingdoms of Castile and Aragon became joined. By the end of the century, they had taken over the Muslim territory of Granada, in the south of Spain, the Kingdom of Navarre in the north, and sent Christopher Columbus on a voyage of discovery that within 50 years saw Spain in control of most of South America, Central America, Florida, Cuba, the West Indies and the Philippines. In 1519, Charles I of Spain, who was related through marriage to the Hapsburg rulers of the Germanic States that made up the Holy Roman Empire, became Charles V, the Holy Roman Emperor, controlling more territory than any other ruler in Europe.

Charles V inherited much of Europe, but he was so exhausted by his rule that he retired to a monastery.

The marriage of Ferdinand and Isabella

The unification of Spain and the wealth from her domination of the New World brought Spain into prominence, beginning in the late fifteenth century.

The Renaissance

Life in the Renaissance | The Political Situation

The English monarchy

In 1485, the Tudor dynasty came to power in England. Henry VII brought the long-running civil war to an end, and prosperity back to the country. His son, Henry VIII, who came to power in 1509, established the Church of England and eliminated the country's allegiance to the Roman Catholic Church, but he also was responsible for the growth of Parliament and the House of Commons. His daughter, Elizabeth I, inherited the throne in 1558, ushering in a period of growth, exploration, prosperity and flowering of the arts in England. She brought stability to the country by ending the religious struggles between Catholics and Protestants, making peace with France and encouraging trade. The defeat of the Spanish Armada, the huge fleet of ships that the King of Spain had sent to attack England, confirmed England's status as a superpower.

Elizabeth I knighted Francis Drake on the deck of his ship, The Golden Hind, for his success in robbing Spanish ships of all their riches.

Henry VIII, by Hans Holbein, 1540

Henry VIII is perhaps best known for having had six wives; two of them were beheaded, a result of Henry's quest for a male heir to inherit the throne.

62 The Renaissance

Society and Culture

Life in the Renaissance

Elizabethan England

Elizabeth I reigned over England for 45 years. During that time, she inspired a dynamic national spirit in her subjects. She restored the people's faith in the monarchy, and generated a climate of self-confidence that brought about an unprecedented period of prosperity. English seafarers during the Elizabethan era made the country a great maritime trading power. The queen had a great interest in the arts and was generous with her support, making the Elizabethan age one of the greatest cultural explosions in English history. Because of her interest in education, 142 new schools were founded during her reign, and the number of students at Oxford and Cambridge increased by 50%. By the end of the Elizabethan era, most of the gentry and merchant class were literate, and nearly half the small landholders. Without this spread of literacy, one of the greatest periods in English literature, which produced poets like Sir Philip Sydney and Edmund Spenser, and playwrights like Christopher Marlowe and William Shakespeare, would never have occurred.

Elizabeth I

A royal procession
Elizabeth is attended by her courtiers and ladies.

An energetic dance at the court of Elizabeth I

Elizabeth I played the lute and the virginals.

The Renaissance

The Reformation

One of the most momentous events of the 1500s was the revolution that took place in the Roman Catholic Church. This revolution, which became known as the Reformation, ended the supremacy of the Pope in Rome and resulted in the birth of Protestantism, a new form of Christianity. The Church had been deeply involved in the politics of Western Europe, and many distrusted its participation in political intrigues and power struggles. Many clergy were no longer remaining true to their vows of chastity and poverty. What upset people most, though, was the scandal over the sale of indulgences. Instead of fasting, going on a pilgrimage or being flogged, sinners could be forgiven for their sins by purchasing indulgences. Often it appeared that someone could buy the spiritual benefit of forgiveness without ever in fact repenting.

Lucas Cranach, *Martin Luther*
Cranach's portrait seems to show Luther's spiritual struggles in his face.

Martin Luther, a German monk and professor of theology, touched off the fire that became the Reformation when he objected to the sale of indulgences to pay for the reconstruction of Saint Peter's Basilica in Rome. On October 31, 1517, he posted his Ninety-five Theses on the door of the Castle Church, Wittenberg. He believed that people did not need to earn God's love by performing good works, going on pilgrimages and buying indulgences. He said that the only authority was the Bible, not the Pope. Luther merely intended to reform the existing Church, but when the pope excommunicated him, Luther formed a parallel Church. Because there were so many more educated people outside the Church who could understand his arguments, his ideas spread all over northern Europe.

In response to the Reformation, the Catholic Church established the Coucil of Trent, which met over an 18-year period to discuss reforms, revitalize the Church and fight Protestantism.

Other branches of Protestantism were begun. The teachings of French lawyer John Calvin were widely accepted in Switzerland and Scotland. In England, the Reformation was more political than religious. Henry VIII wanted to divorce his first wife and remarry in order to get a male heir. When the Pope refused him, Henry renounced the Pope's authority and established the Church of England, with himself as the head. His reforms included the creation of a liturgy in English and dissolving the monasteries. To this day, the head of the Church of England is the reigning monarch.

Society and Culture

Life in the Renaissance

Voyages of discovery

In the late fifteenth and sixteenth century, Europeans began to explore uncharted areas of the globe in search of the route to China and the riches of the East. The explorers themselves were undoubtedly inspired by a spirit of adventure and scientific curiosity, but those who funded their explorations had rather different motivations. The voyages were either underwritten by kings and queens who wanted to expand their country's influence and fill their coffers in the process, or by merchant groups who wanted to find new sources of trade goods and further their business interests. No matter what the motivation, however, these explorations brought many changes to the nations that spawned them.

The most famous of all the explorers was Christopher Columbus, who sailed west from Spain into unknown territory, discovering San Salvador, Cuba and Hispaniola in what is now called the West Indies. But there were others as well. Portugal was one of the major exploring nations. In 1497, Vasco da Gama sailed down the west coast of Africa, around the southern tip and up to India, where he traded for spices and precious gems. Within 20 years, the Portuguese had sailed all the way to China.

Other explorers followed Columbus to the New World. Spain expanded its influence in the Americas with Juan Ponce de León's explorations in Florida and the Yucatan, Hernán Cortés' destruction of the Aztec empire in Mexico, and Franciso Pizarro's victory over the Incas of Peru. An expedition led by Fernand de Magellan, the Portuguese-born Spanish explorer and navigator, was the first to sail completely around the world. By the middle of the sixteenth century, Spain was immensely rich and controlled the West Indies, Cuba, Florida, Mexico, Central America, much of South America, and the Philippines.

Portugal and Spain were the leaders, but other countries too sent adventurers on voyages of discovery. John Cabot sailed to Labrador, Newfoundland and New England for the English in 1497. In 1534 and 1535, French explorer Jacques Cartier made two trips to North America for Francis I. He sailed around Newfoundland and into the Gulf of the St. Lawrence on the first trip, and explored the St. Lawrence River as far as present-day Montreal on the second, thus laying the basis for the French Empire in North America. English explorers included Sir Francis Drake, who circumnavigated the globe between 1578 and 1580, and Sir Walter Raleigh, who tried in 1585 to establish a colony on Roanoke Island in what is now North Carolina. The English East India company was set up in 1600 to establish a spice and silk trade with the Orient.

Fernand de Magellan
Magellan died before completing his voyage around the world, but one of his ships continued westward until it reached Spain, thus proving that the world is round.

No contemporary portraits were ever made of Columbus, so all the pictures we have of him are done from the imagination.

A picture of Columbus' ships, the *Niña*, the *Pinta* and the *Santa Maria*

Jacques Cartier was in search of the Northwest passage to the Pacific when he explored the St. Lawrence River.

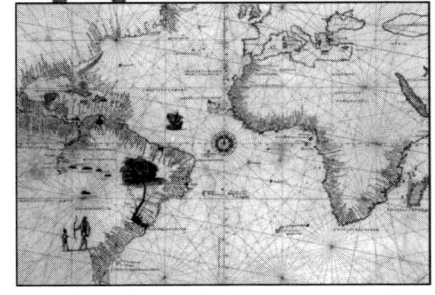

This map made in 1553 shows how well charted the Atlantic coasts of Africa and Central and South America were.

The Renaissance 65

Life in the Renaissance
Society and Culture

How the upper classes lived

With the increase in commerce, trade and production of goods that came during the Renaissance, there were a growing number of wealthy people who could enjoy the kind of lifestyle that had previously been only within reach of the nobility. This was particularly true in Italy. In addition to the powerful families running the various city states, there were also rich merchants and traders. These people were primarily urban and a palace in the city suited their needs perfectly. Often occupying a whole block, these palaces might be built in a square around a central courtyard. The lower level could house offices, shops and warehouses in addition to the stables, and the windows were often small and barred against attackers. The living space was on the second and third floors, which had larger windows with shutters that could be closed against the weather and civil disturbances. The palace concept spread from Italy throughout Europe. In France, the idea was combined with the mediaeval castle to produce the country *château*.

Wealthy Italians also needed an escape from the city in the heat of the summer, so the idea of a villa in the country became popular. The villa might be in the country on an estate that could provide produce for the house in town, growing wheat for bread, olives for oil, and grapes for wine. Or it might just be a suburban villa, a quiet place for a weekend retreat.

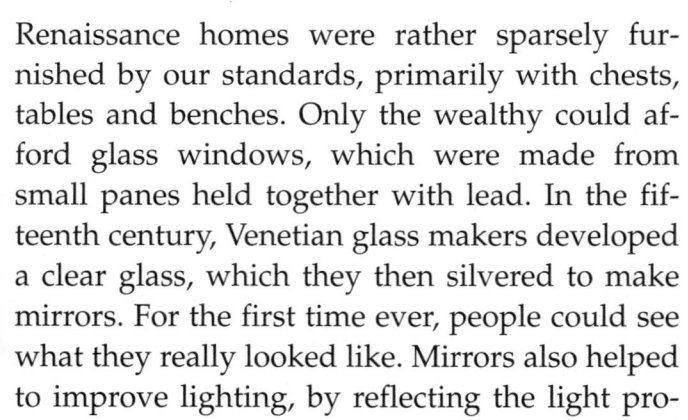

Renaissance homes were rather sparsely furnished by our standards, primarily with chests, tables and benches. Only the wealthy could afford glass windows, which were made from small panes held together with lead. In the fifteenth century, Venetian glass makers developed a clear glass, which they then silvered to make mirrors. For the first time ever, people could see what they really looked like. Mirrors also helped to improve lighting, by reflecting the light produced by candles and oil lamps. Another innovation was the table fork, which was introduced from the East. In the Middle Ages, people ate with a knife and their fingers; now beautifully decorated forks were being used in upper-class homes.

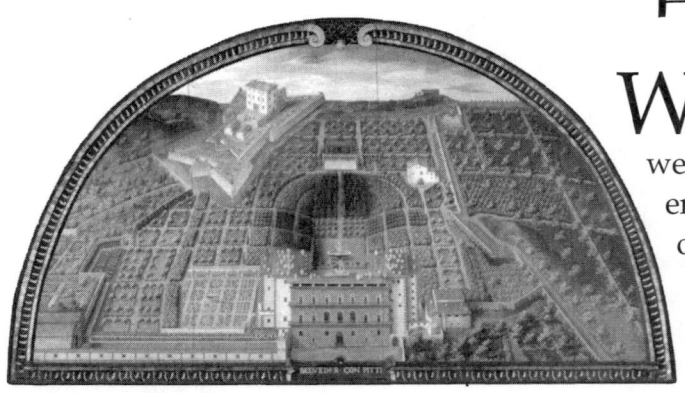

The Pitti Palace in Florence
It was built for the Pitti family, but later purchased by the Medici. They were responsible for the extensive landscaping, and the Boboli gardens behind the palace.

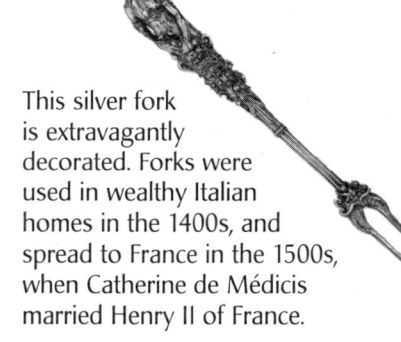

This silver fork is extravagantly decorated. Forks were used in wealthy Italian homes in the 1400s, and spread to France in the 1500s, when Catherine de Médicis married Henry II of France.

The château of Chambord combines the idea of a castle with the concept of the Italian palace.

Society and Culture | Life in the Renaissance

How the poorer people lived

Peasants and the urban poor were not much better off in the Renaissance than they were in the Middle Ages. In fact, the poor city dwellers might not be as well off as the country people, because they were often in dwellings that were crowded and unsanitary, without even clean country air to breathe. However, in some respects their situation was better: they were not tied to one piece of land and one landowner, they had opportunities other than farming and it was possible to make a little money. A young boy could be apprenticed to a craftsman and be trained as a leather worker, glassmaker or weaver, for example, working his way up to becoming a salaried journeyman, and perhaps even a master, able to take on apprentices himself.

This picture of a tailor's shop shows three workmen. The one standing at the table is undoubtedly the most experienced one of the three, because no one without a lot of training would have been allowed to do anything as risky as cutting the cloth.

These peasants are taking a lunch break while one of their number continues to cut grain in the background.

This painting shows an idealized version of the peasant's life. These workers are happily engaged in picking grapes and crushing them to begin the process of making wine. Every one, rich and poor, drank great quantities of wine— it was safer to drink than the water.

The Renaissance

Life in the Renaissance

Society and Culture

Renaissance dress

Clothing styles typical of the Renaissance began in the late fifteenth century in Italy, of course, and then spread to the rest of Europe. In the first half of the sixteenth century, the Germans and the Flemish were the trend setters, and after 1550, Spain had the primary influence.

The Italian style for men in the early Renaissance involved a white silk or linen shirt, with frills at the neck and wrists. Over this, they wore a short tunic and tight fitting hose. Older men wore a long gown over top, with a decorative lining that showed when the edges were turned back. Women's dresses had a low, square-cut neckline that emphasized the bust, which might be made more modest with a covering of transparent fabric. Sleeves were large, and the skirts fell in folds to the ground.

By the 1520s, the German fashion for slashings had become all the rage. The top layer of a garment was slashed to allow the colour of the fabric beneath to show through. Men wore a longer tunic, called a doublet, which opened in the front to display a prominent codpiece. Women's figures were constrained by boned bodices. They also wore farthingales, underskirts with hoops of whalebone that held the dress out from the body. Fashionable headdresses were hoods attached to jewelled metal frames, worn over caps that almost completely concealed the hair.

A portrait of Lucrecia Panciatichi, 1550-60, by Bronzino

This dress shows the effect of a boned bodice. The skirt and the sleeves are both slashed.

Jane Seymour, the third wife of Henry VIII. Notice her headdress.

This grouping of men in different outfits shows the range of possibilities for men in the early Renaissance.

68 The Renaissance

Society and Culture

Life in the Renaissance

Renaissance dress

In the last half of the sixteenth century, fashions for both men and women of wealth became more extreme and very luxurious. Fabrics were encrusted with jewels and embroidery, with lots of patterns. Spain was extremely rich as a result of the explorations in the New World, and styles from Spain were in vogue all over Europe. Men's doublets were now fitted to the waist and buttoned down the front. They wore what were called trunk hose, which were mid-thigh-length breeches gathered into waist and thigh bands. Capes of various lengths were worn.

Women's fashions got even more uncomfortable in the last half of the century. The boned bodice evolved into a tight corset and the farthingale became wider. The French introduced the wheel farthingale, which was drum-shaped. Dresses also called for stomachers, stiff, padded V-shaped panels which reached down well below the waist. Ruffs became fashionable for both sexes. They were made from a band of fabric that tied around the neck. Another strip of material was sewn to the band in ruffles. When starch was introduced after 1565, the ruffs became larger, because the starch helped them to stay stiff.

The poorer people wore clothes that were simpler and made of ordinary, easily available materials, like rough wools. The basic shapes were similar to the clothing of the wealthy classes, but there was nothing luxurious about them.

The Archduke Ferdinand of Tyrol is wearing slashed trunk hose with an elaborate padded codpiece and a short doublet.

This gentleman has a slashed doublet and a short Spanish cape.

Sir Walter Raleigh and his son

Notice how the boy is dressed in a similar style to his father.

This portrait of the Infante Isabelle Claire Eugénie of Spain shows her dress with a stomacher and a skirt held out with a bell-shaped farthingale.

Both mother and child are wearing ruffs here.

This rather fanciful portrait of Elizabeth I shows her wearing a dress with a wheel farthingale.

The Renaissance

Life in the Renaissance   Science and Thought

The growth of literacy

During the Middle Ages, literacy was not widespread. In general, the only people who could read and write were the clergy and the nobility, and not all of them. Scholarship, studying classical texts and other intellectual activities were only carried out by the clergy, usually members of monastic orders. In the Renaissance, however, there began to be many more educated lay people. New schools and private tutors encouraged the study of Latin and Greek so that the original classical texts could be read. Universities that had been established in the Middle Ages, like Bologna, Paris, Oxford and Cambridge, added degrees in the humanities to the ones they already offered in law, medicine and theology.

To this climate of interest in literature and ideas was added the invention of the printing press. The Chinese had developed movable type in the eleventh century, but Johannes Gutenberg was the first to cast movable type in metal. He also invented a machine that could print a page of text from the type set into a form and produce 300 copies a day. His first complete printed book was a copy of the Bible, produced in 1455. For the first time, books were not just available to the clergy or the aristocracy, who could afford manuscript copies. The subject matter became broader too. Religious and classical works were important still, but a much wider range of literature became available. Books became entertaining as well as instructive or uplifting.

Cambridge University in England

Gutenberg displays a page that is just off the press.

The printing press also allowed works of literature to reach a wider public. William Caxton's edition of Chaucer's *Canterbury Tales* was published in 1483.

This picture illustrates a print shop, where the printers are preparing type and pressing pages.

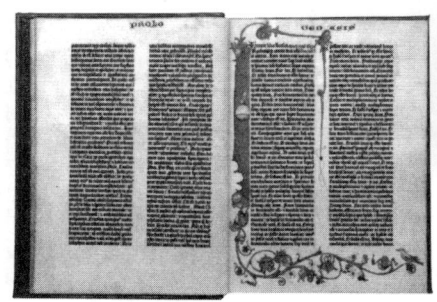

The Gutenberg Bible, Gutenberg's first complete book, was produced in 1455.

70   The Renaissance

Science and Thought

Life in the Renaissance

Humanism

Humanism, in connection with the Renaissance, refers to the study of ancient literature, history and moral philosophy, and it is not surprising that it developed in Italy where people lived among reminders of ancient Roman civilization. It was not that the classical works from Rome and Greece were unknown in the Middle Ages, because it was the monks in the scriptoria who saved them. But in the Renaissance they were studied by lay people, who did not automatically see things from a religious point of view. Humanism was essentially a program for education which involved the study of grammar, rhetoric, history, poetry and moral philosophy as found in ancient Latin and Greek texts, and was seen as the way to produce good citizens. It became the main intellectual force in Renaissance Italy and spread to most of Europe.

Erasmus, painted by Hans Holbein

Humanism focussed more on life on earth than on the promise of a life in heaven. More emphasis was placed on individual achievement and human feeling, less reliance on tradition and religious authority. Its influence was felt in the growth of literature in the language spoken by the people instead of Latin, as well as in the writing of history, art and the way people lived their lives.

One of the most important humanist thinkers was the Dutch cleric and scholar Desiderius Erasmus (c. 1469-1536). He studied and lectured all over Western Europe and made several trips to England, establishing humanism there as well. His criticism of corruption in the Catholic Church preceded the Reformation, although he was not really a religious reformer. He also held enlightened views about education and teaching children; he criticized excessive discipline and encouraged arousing the children's interest. His most famous work is *In Praise of Folly*.

A page from *In Praise of Folly* with a drawing by Hans Holbein

Niccolò Machiavelli (1469-1527) was a political philosopher who was raised in the Italian humanist tradition but who reached very different moral conclusions. *The Prince* was a statement of Machiavelli's philosophy of politics, which he developed during his career as a diplomat in Florence. According to Machiavelli, the ideal leader, or prince, is a benevolent despot for whom the preservation of the state is the only goal. The book describes the various unscrupulous methods by which a ruler can gain and hold power. To this day, a cunning schemer may be called "machiavellian."

Niccolò Machiavelli

The Renaissance 71

A revolution in astronomy

The Greek astronomer Ptolemy had defined the universe back in the second century. He said that the Earth was the centre of the universe and the planets and the sun revolve around the Earth. This Earth-centred view was universally accepted, particularly by the Church, which saw proof in this system that God designed the universe for the benefit of human beings alone.

In 1543, the Polish astronomer Nicolas Copernicus (1473-1543) published *De Revolutionibus Orbium Coelestium* (*On the Revolution of the Celestial Spheres*) in which he theorized that in fact the Earth revolves on its own axis once a day and around the sun once a year. He said that the planets too revolve around the sun and the Earth wobbles like a top as it rotates. Copernicus knew that the Church would raise objections to his work, so he had waited 26 years after developing his theories to publish them. He died shortly after that and never knew the impact of his work. No longer could man consider himself the centre of the universe.

About 50 years later, the Italian astronomer and physicist Galileo Galilei (1564-1642) began to study the Copernican theory. He also began to build telescopes. When he succeeded in making one that magnified everything 20 times, he discovered that, contrary to popular belief, the moon had a rough surface and the Milky Way was made up of individual stars. He also discovered the four moons of Jupiter. These earth-shattering discoveries were seen by the Church as heresy. Galileo maintained that no scientific theory should be designated as an article of faith, but his writings were censored and he was forced to stand trial for heresy before the Inquisition. Galileo had to renounce his theories and was sentenced to house arrest for the rest of his life. Galileo's scientific studies were important, but perhaps his most significant contribution was his effort to liberate scientific enquiry from obstruction by received philosophical and theological ideas.

This model of Ptolemy's conception of the universe shows the Earth at the centre and the paths of the planets encircling the earth as different rings around it.

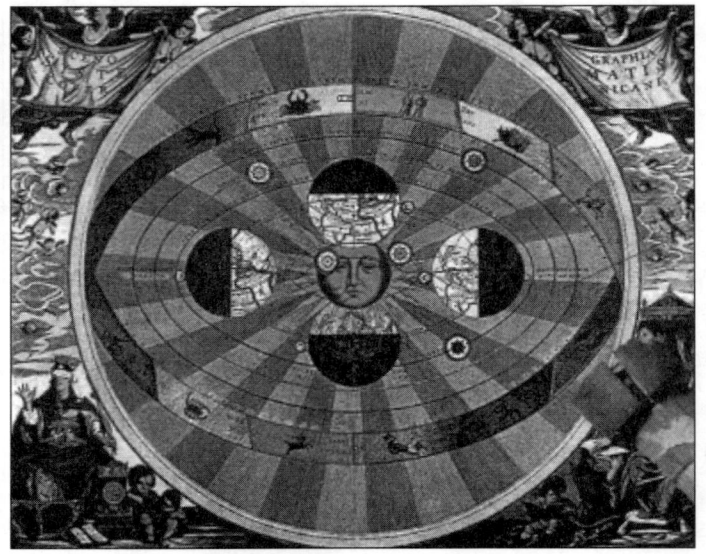

The Copernican System shows the sun at the centre and the different planets on rings around it, in order according to the length of time it took them to go around their orbit.

Life in the Renaissance

Invention timeline

1444   Portugal began the modern slave trade, bringing Africans to work as agricultural labourers.

1450   Johannes Gutenberg developed the first printing press. He made metal casts of the letters of the alphabet, put them together to form words and sentences, rolled them with oily ink, and pressed them onto a piece of paper. He could print thousands of copies very quickly.

1470   Navigators began to make use of smaller versions of the astrolabe to mark a ship's position at sea.

1504   German armourers invented an acid etching process to help them decorate the heavily engraved armour that was then fashionable. This knowledge was later used for etching printing plates.

1520   Spanish explorer Cortés was served a drink made of chocolate in Mexico and introduced it to Spain.

1538   Diving bells were used in Spain. They were cylinders that were open at one end so that when they were lowered into the water, a bubble of air remained in the closed end. Divers could work underwater until the oxygen in the air ran out.

1556   Tobacco grown in the New World was brought back to Spain. It was introduced into France the same year. Sir Francis Drake brought it to England in 1581.

1569   Gerhard Mercator, a Flemish geographer, developed a way of drawing maps that solved the problems that navigators encountered when they tried to map a round world on a flat piece of paper. The Mercator projection allowed them to plot an accurate course.

1590   Dutch eyeglass maker Hans Jensen invented the compound microscope to enable the eye to see very small objects. Jensen also put together a telescope by following an Italian design. Galileo was the first to use telescopes in the study of astronomy in 1609.

1592   Galileo invented a thermometer made of a tube of air in a container of coloured liquid. When the air warmed up, it pushed the level of the liquid down.

A printing press, showing the stone slab that held the type and the ink ball used to spread ink on the type. The printer slid the slab under the press, which was lowered to press the image of the type onto the paper.

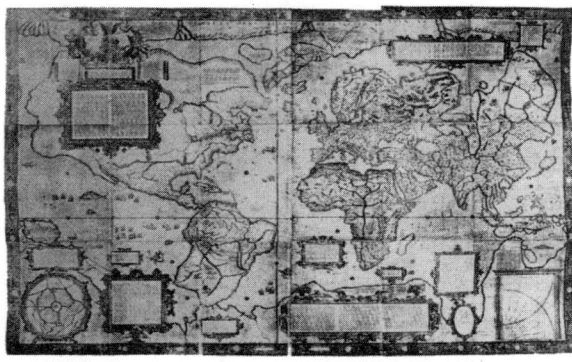

An astrolabe

A map drawn using the Mercator projection

The Renaissance

The Arts in the Renaissance

Literature

English literature

The last half of the sixteenth century, during the reign of Elizabeth I, was the beginning of a golden age in English literature. It was the time in which England absorbed the European Renaissance, and there were a number of writers of genius who contributed to the brilliance of this literary century.

Two important late sixteenth-century poets were Sir Philip Sidney (1554-86) and Edmund Spenser (c. 1552-99), who were courtiers to Queen Elizabeth. In his sonnet cycle, *Astrophel and Stella,* Sidney did much to develop the Italian sonnet form in English, and Spenser's *The Faerie Queen* is a blend of mediaeval allegory and romantic epic. The Faerie Queen, Gloriana, symbolized Queen Elizabeth, and each of the books in the poem represents a moral quality couched as the virtuous quest of one of her knights.

But if poetry flourished in these years in England, drama was the focal point of the age. Drama spoke to everyone, from the poor people who stood through the theatre performances, to the sophisticated playgoers who saw the plays performed at court. It was a blend of upper-class humanistic ideas and the popular taste for spectacle. Christopher Marlowe (1564-93), the first major Elizabethan playwright, wrote such tragedies as *Tamburlaine, Doctor Faustus,* and *The Jew of Malta.* The genius of the Elizabethan theatre was, however, William Shakespeare (1564-1616), a figure who has towered over English literature for 400 years. Shakespeare's rich style has great power and poetry—he has contributed more expressions to the English language than any other writer. His plots are complex, and he deals with universal human emotions and conflicts. His comedies examine the laughable aspects of human nature as well as the charming ones, while his tragedies study the basic reasons for human action: love, jealousy, ambition, heroism, revenge. Perhaps the best loved comedies are *As You Like It, Twelfth Night* and *Much Ado about Nothing,* while the tragedies that continue to stir us include *Hamlet, Romeo and Juliet, Macbeth, Othello,* and *King Lear.*

A portrait of Shakespeare

The Globe Theatre, where Shakespeare's plays were performed

It burned down in 1613 and was rebuilt in 1614 only to be destroyed 30 years later by the Puritans.

There were no women actors in the Elizabethan theatre. The female roles were all played by boys.

A reconstruction of the Globe Theatre interior

74 The Renaissance

Literature

The Arts in the Renaissance

French literature

There were several important poets of the French Renaissance. Clément Marot (1496-1594) was in the service of Francis I, and as such was exposed to the influence of Italian humanism. His wit and graceful style made his work popular even though he was imprisoned for heresy. His best known poem is *L'Enfer*, an allegory on justice that he wrote while in exile. After Marot's death, there arose a group of poets, called La Pléiade after a group of Greek poets, whose aim was to create French poetry that was comparable in quality to that of the ancients. Chief among them was Pierre de Ronsard (1524-85). Many of his odes illustrate his love of nature, and tell of unrequited love and the brevity of youth and beauty. He was a master of the 12-syllable alexandrine, the verse line that is as characteristic of French poetry as iambic pentameter is of English. His *Amours de Cassandre* were strongly influenced by the Italian poet Petrarch.

The writings of François Rabelais (c. 1493-1553) were an important forum for humanist ideas. His most famous works are the comic epic stories he wrote about giants called *Pantagruel and Gargantua*. His earthy humour and talent for satirizing society made his works extremely popular. Diametrically opposed in style are the *Essais* of Michel de Montaigne (1538-92), a humanist and scholar who wrote of his personal philosophy on many different matters. Montaigne investigated ideas with an open mind, and revered rationality.

Italian drama

One of the earliest forms of professional theatre, called commedia dell'arte, developed in Italy in the 1500s and was extremely popular there for at least 200 years. Theatre troupes of six to twelve men and women improvised commedia dell'arte plays, using a series of stock characters, slapstick humour and clowning. All the characters wore identifying masks. Commedia dell'arte spread to other countries, and the familiar characters, like the beautiful young girl, the cheeky servant, the pedantic professor and the husband whose wife is cheating on him, all may be found in modern day plays and films. Their improvisational nature is something that was handed down as well. Many composers, artists and playwrights have drawn inspiration from the commedia dell'arte.

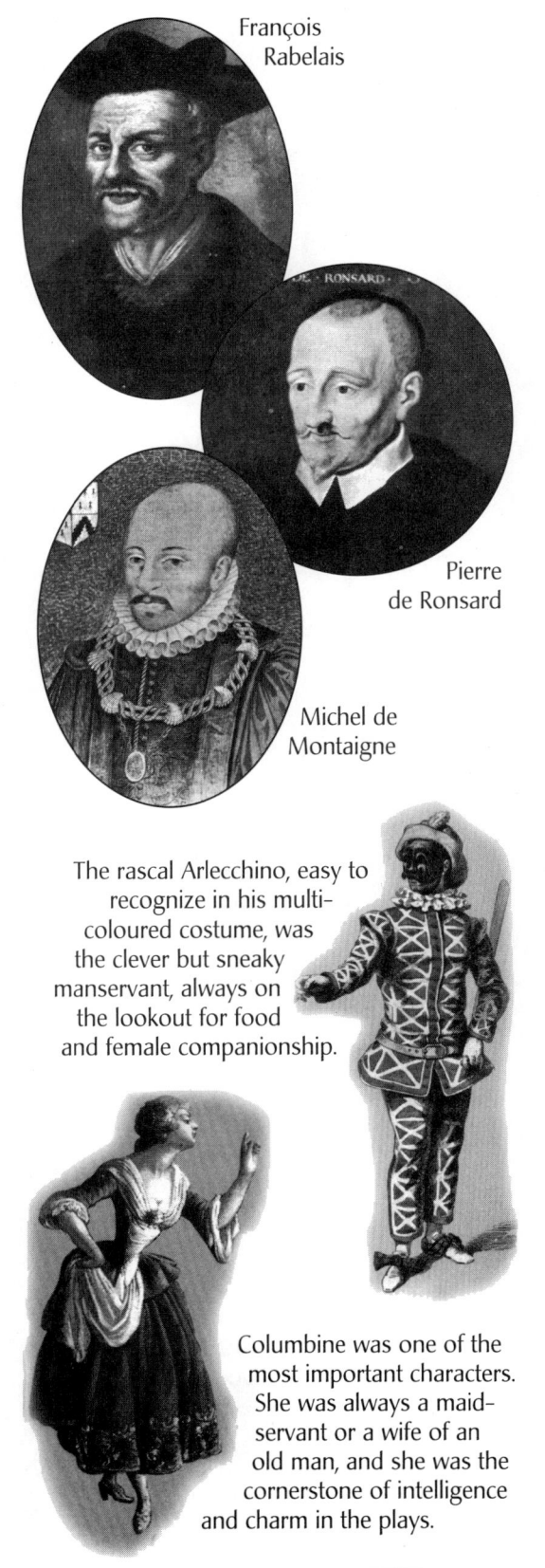

François Rabelais

Pierre de Ronsard

Michel de Montaigne

The rascal Arlecchino, easy to recognize in his multi-coloured costume, was the clever but sneaky manservant, always on the lookout for food and female companionship.

Columbine was one of the most important characters. She was always a maid-servant or a wife of an old man, and she was the cornerstone of intelligence and charm in the plays.

The Renaissance

The Arts in the Renaissance — Architecture

A return to antiquity

The architects of the Renaissance returned to the buildings of Greece and Rome for their inspiration. They applied classical design principles and turned away from pointed arches, flying buttresses and ribbed vaulting in favour of the round arch, the barrel vault, the column and the dome. Everything was built according to the mathematical proportions that had been declared harmonious by the Romans and Greeks.

The first great Italian architect of the Renaissance was Filippo Brunelleschi and the first great centre of architecture was Florence. In 1402, Brunelleschi won the competition to complete the dome for the cathedral in Florence. It was a huge dome and could not be built with mediaeval methods. Brunelleschi reinvented a solution used by the Romans, which involved using bricks in a herringbone pattern within a stone framework. The double-walled structure crowned with a lantern still dominates the skyline in Florence.

About this time, prominent people like the Medici in Florence were asking for a different kind of urban residence, which became known as a palazzo. A palazzo was several stories high, built around a central courtyard that was open to the sky. The lower level was for offices and work spaces and the upper levels were for living. Architects also began building villas in the country, an old Roman practice that enabled people to get away from the heat of the city.

Filippo Brunelleschi

Brunelleschi's dome on top of the cathedral in Florence

The Medici Palazzo in Florence was built in the 1440s by Michelozzo, a student of Brunelleschi. Each level of the building has a different finish, beginning with rough-hewn masonry on the bottom and moving to much finer work on the top.

Architecture

The Arts in the Renaissance

A return to antiquity

In the sixteenth century, the architectural centre moved from Florence to Rome. The leading architect was Donato Bramante, and his Tempietto, or "little temple," built in 1502 to mark the site of St. Peter's crucifixion, was one of the earliest Renaissance structures in Rome. Bramante received the commission to rebuild the Vatican church of St. Peter's from Pope Julius II. He designed a huge structure based on a Greek cross, which has two intersecting arms of the same length, as opposed to the traditional design based on the Latin cross, which produces a long centre aisle and a shorter one in the other direction. He also revived the technology of making concrete, lost since Roman times. Bramante died in 1514 before construction had progressed very far, and for the next 30 years various architects worked at carrying out his design. The mutilfaceted artist Michelangelo, who was also an architect, brought the project to completion, incorporating his own ideas into Bramante's basic plan.

Later in the sixteenth century, the architect Andrea Palladio was active in the area around Venice. His most important works are a number of country villas. His ideas on architecture spread after he published his treatise, *Four Books on Architecture*.

Evidence of the spread of Renaissance architecture outside Italy is found in the French château of Fontainebleau, built for Francis I.

St. Peter's Basilica and the Vatican, Rome

Bramante's Tempietto
Janson

The dome on St. Peter's, begun in 1547

Palladio's most famous work is the Villa Rotunda in Vicenza built in 1567-70. It is absolutely square, topped with a dome, and each of the four sides has an identical porch like the front of a temple.

The Renaissance

The early Renaissance

The dominant sculptor of the early Renaissance was Donatello, who worked primarily in Florence. Donatello recaptured the classical way of portraying the body as though it was made of real bones and muscle, capable of movement. His statue of St. George begun in 1415 shows the warrior saint poised for action, so that we can feel the tension as he waits for the enemy to appear. Another of Donatello's innovations was the relief work below the statue. He devised a way of carving a series of planes for the background that give an illusion of depth. The figures carved in high relief in the foreground stand out against background forms that are carved in increasingly lower relief, so that they appear to be more distant. St. George is set in a niche in the church of the Or San Michele, but with his statue of David, Donatello produced the first free-standing sculpture since ancient times.

Another important early Renaissance sculptor was Lorenzo Ghiberti. Ghiberti's gilded bronze doors for the Baptistery in Florence are considered his masterpiece. Called *The Gates of Paradise*, they consist of ten panels illustrating scenes from the Old Testament, which are almost like paintings, with the figures shown in a landscape or against architecture in perspective, giving a greater sense of depth than is actually there.

Donatello, St. *George Tabernacle*, 1415-17

Note the relief work underneath the statue.

Donatello, *David*, 1425-30

Donatello has again caught the moment that the figure is at rest, with all his weight on one leg. The sculptor has emphasized David's weakness by modelling an adolescent boy rather than a heavily muscled man, and giving him a wreathed hat, in contrast to Goliath's warrior helmet.

Lorenzo Ghiberti, *The Gates of Paradise*, 1435

Sculpture

The Arts in the Renaissance

The later Renaissance

Michelangelo dominates the sculpture of the High Renaissance, as perhaps he does the sculpture of all time. He was a painter and architect as well as a sculptor, but it was in the works he carved from marble that his greatest artistry is revealed. He saw himself as a real creator, releasing the bodies he chiselled from their stone prisons. His huge statue of David, in the moment just before he faces the killer Goliath, has a body of godlike beauty and a face that is truly human, showing anxiety in the furrowed brow, alertness in the steady gaze, all combined with an intensity of purpose as he seems to be sizing up the enemy. Similarly, the statue of Moses carved for the tomb of Pope Julius II seems to show a man who is both vigilant and thoughtful, someone who could be wise and at the same time capable of great wrath.

During the late Renaissance, some sculptors adopted a more stylized approach. The goldsmith Benvenuto Cellini is best known for the golden salt cellar he made for King Francis I of France, with two elongated figures, one representing Neptune, king of the sea, and the other an embodiment of the earth.

Primaticcio was another sculptor who worked for Francis I. He was strongly influenced by the painter Parmigianino, and his sculptures in stucco for many of the main rooms at the château at Fontainebleau have the same kind of stylized artificiality.

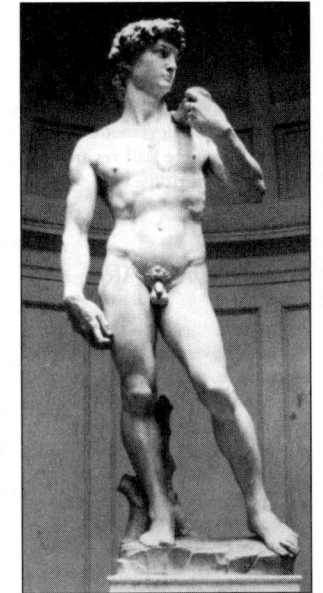

Michelangelo, *David*, 1501-4

The figure of David is 13.5 feet (about 4 metres) high.

Michelangelo, *Moses*, 1513-15

Benvenuto Cellini, *The Saltcellar of Francis I*, 1539-43

Since salt comes from the ocean, Cellini modelled a little boat to hold it, and since pepper comes from the earth, the pepper is in a tiny triumphal arch watched over by the earth goddess.

Michelangelo, *Pièta*, 1498-1500

One of Michelangelo's most famous works, this statue of the Virgin Mary cradling the dead Christ in her arms is in St. Peters Basilica, Rome.

The Arts in the Renaissance
Painting

The early Renaissance

Renaissance painting is dramatically different from the painting of the Middle Ages. Where mediaeval painters presented their ideas as symbols, Renaissance artists aimed for realism. Mediaeval painters gave us stereotypes, but the Renaissance painter was interested in individual people, and developed the ability to illustrate a figure's character. In the Middle Ages, artists organized space in succeeding planes, whereas in the Renaissance, they learned to paint a scene with depth, as it is seen by the eye. Renaissance artists also rediscovered the beauty of the human form, giving it the reverence that mediaeval artists reserved for God alone.

The architect Filippo Brunelleschi redeveloped the principles of linear perspective that had been understood, at least crudely, by the Romans. Linear perspective is the phenomenon by which objects grow smaller and closer together as they recede into the distance, as railroad tracks become narrower and closer together finally converging at the vanishing point, the point on the horizon where all parallel lines converge. These developments meant that Renaissance artists were able to portray the world as it is, and they were much more interested in painting realistic landscapes. Northern Renaissance artists, especially those in Holland and Flanders, were particularly influential in the development of aerial perspective, in which objects appear to fade and become blurrier as they recede from the viewer's eye.

One of the first masters of the early Renaissance was Masaccio. The frescoes he painted in the Brancacci Chapel in Florence are his masterpieces. In *The Expulsion of Adam and Eve from the Garden of Eden*, Adam and Eve are real people in anguish. *The Tribute Money* (1427) is a breakthrough in the portrayal of natural light and perspective. The most important works of Piero della Francesca (1416-92) are the many frescoes in the church of San Francesco in Arezzo, Italy, telling the legend of the True Cross, that is, the cross used for Christ's crucifixion. The lyric, flowing works of Sandro Botticelli (1444-1510), made him the favoured painter of Lorenzo the Magnificent and his circle in Florence. Another influential early Renaissance painter was Andrea Mantegna (1431-1506).

Masaccio, The Expulsion of Adam and Eve, 1427

Painting | The Arts in the Renaissance

The early Renaissance

Masaccio, *The Tribute Money*, 1427

Mantegna, *St. James led to his execution*, 1455

The unusual "worm's eye view" causes the architecture to dominate the scene.

The Discovery and Proving of the True Cross, one of the frescoes in the church of San Francesco by Piero della Francesca

Sandro Botticelli, *Primavera* (Spring)

Sandro Botticelli, *The Birth of Venus*

Botticelli's Venus seems to fuse the goddess of love with the ethereal beauty of a Madonna.

The Renaissance 81

The Arts in the Renaissance — Painting

The High Renaissance

The painters of the Italian High Renaissance are some of the most famous artists in the history of the world; they include Leonardo da Vinci, Michelangelo, Raphael, Giorgione, Titian.

Leonardo da Vinci was a painter, sculptor, engineer, architect and scientist. He produced perhaps the most recognizable painting in the world, the *Mona Lisa*. Another of his famous works, *The Last Supper*, a fresco in the monastery of Santa Maria delle Grazie in Milan, is a masterpiece of perspective. The sight lines all draw the viewer's eye to the figure of Christ. In his later years, Leonardo devoted himself to scientific interests. His anatomical drawings combine scientific curiosity with his artist's ability to observe and record. He created the concept of the modern scientific illustration.

Michelangelo was another multifaceted genius. He was a painter as well as a sculptor and architect. His masterworks in painting are undoubtedly the frescos on the ceiling of the Sistine Chapel in the Vatican in Rome commissioned by Pope Julius II. The ceiling, some ten thousand square feet in area, took him four years to complete. The frescoes tell the stories of the Bible's book of Genesis, with over three hundred figures, some larger than life size.

Leonardo da Vinci, *Mona Lisa*, 1503-5

People down through the ages have admired the Mona Lisa's smile and her aura of mystery.

Leonardo da Vinci, *The Last Supper*, 1495-98

Leonardo used a new fresco technique for *The Last Supper* that did not adhere well to the wall, and it began to deteriorate only three years after it was finished. Restoration work done during the 1990s has restored some of the original colour to the fresco, which has been decaying for over 400 years.

Michelangelo, *The Creation of Adam*, 1508-12

God, having created man in his own image, reaches over and gives him the spark of life.

Painting

The Arts in the Renaissance

The High Renaissance

Raphael was another painter whose work was commissioned by Pope Julius II. *The School of Athens* was one of a cycle of frescoes Raphael produced when he was asked to decorate the pope's library in his private apartments in the Vatican. It is seen as his masterpiece. Illustrating the theme of philosophy, the two central figures, the Greek philosophers Plato and Aristotle, are surrounded by other philosophers engaged in argument.

Giorgione is known for his paintings of figures set in idyllic landscapes. His pastoral nudes ushered in a new theme in European art. No longer was it necessary to tell a story; the beauty of the landscape and the human figure were enough.

Titian, influenced by Giorgione, continued the tradition of figures in an idyllic landscape. He also became the most sought-after portrait painter of his time. He is famous for his technique with oils, and his use of colour, vivid reds and golden yellows.

Raphael, *The School of Athens*, 1510-11
Many of the figures in the fresco are portraits of Raphael's contemporaries.

Raphael, *Parnassus*, 1511
This fresco surrounding a door is another in the cycle of frescoes Raphael painted for Pope Julius II. Its theme is poetry.

Giorgione, *Fête champêtre*

Titian, *Bacchus and Ariadne*, 1520

The Renaissance 83

The late Renaissance

In the late Renaissance, there was a reaction to the style of the High Renaissance; this new movement came to be called mannerism. The earliest mannerist painters pulled away from the classicism of the High Renaissance. Fiorentino's *Descent from the Cross*, for example, shows sharp edges and acid colours that are very different from the flowing lines and naturalism of the previous generation of Renaissance painters.

The Madonna with the Long Neck by Parmigianino is typical of mannerist style, with elongated bodies in exaggerated poses and a general sense of artificiality.

One of the greatest mannerist painters was Tintoretto, who used the tactic of contrasting bright light and deep darkness to increase the drama of his works. He also often organized his paintings on a diagonal that reaches to the very back of the scene, another theatrical technique. One of his greatest works, *The Last Supper*, is very different from the painting of the same name by Leonardo da Vinci.

Rosso Fiorentino, *Descent from the Cross*, 1521

Parmigianino, *The Madonna with the Long Neck*, 1535

Tintoretto, *The Last Supper*, 1592-94

Tintoretto often included elements of the supernatural in his works. Here, angels conjured from the clouds of smoke from the oil lamp seem to hover over the table.

Painting

The late Renaissance

El Greco was a Spanish painter who worked in the mannerist style. Originally from Crete (El Greco is Spanish for "the Greek"), he studied in Venice under Titian and Tintoretto before moving to Spain. His best known work is the *Burial of Count Orgaz*, an illustration of the fourteenth-century miracle in which Jesus Christ, the Virgin Mary and St. John appeared at the funeral to receive the soul of Count Orgaz.

Not all artists in the late Renaissance were mannerists. Veronese, for instance, a Venetian painter who was second in importance there only to Tintoretto, is more likely to be called a realist. In *Feast in the House of Levi*, he shows a cityscape populated with real people, portraits of contemporary upper-class Venetians, with a mass of detail including dogs and drunkards. Originally entitled *The Last Supper*, Veronese was called up before the Inquisition for the impropriety of including such vulgarities in a religious picture.

Corregio was an artist who worked primarily in Parma. His naturalism and use of light and shade was an inspiration to seventeenth-century Baroque painters. He is well-known for his religious paintings, small devotional works as well as great altarpieces, and a number of lyrically sensuous mythological paintings.

El Greco, *Burial of Count Orgaz*, 1586

The painting is huge, hung above the Count's actual burial site, and the heavenly vision that occupies the top half of the picture dominates the space.

Corregio, *Jupiter and Io*, 1532

In this mythological painting, the nymph Io swoons in the embrace of the god Jupiter, who comes to her in the form of a huge thundercloud.

Veronese, *Feast in the House of Levi*, 1573

The Arts in the Renaissance — Painting

Renaissance painting in Northern Europe

Rogier van der Weyden, *Descent from the Cross*, 1435

The Renaissance painters of Northern Europe were not nearly as influenced by antiquity as the Italians. Nor were they as affected by the discovery of perspective, or the scientific analysis of the human body as were the Italian painters. Rogier van der Weyden was a Flemish artist who was influenced by Jan van Eyck, but whose primary interest was communicating emotional drama. His masterwork is the *Descent from the Cross*, which illustrates all the grief suffered by the followers of Jesus as they took him down from the cross. Another Flemish masterwork is the *Portinari Altarpiece* painted by Hugo van der Goes. The huge three-panel altarpiece depicts the shepherds excitedly coming to worship the baby Jesus, with the Portinari family, who commissioned the work, in the side panels.

Hieronymus Bosch was a Dutch painter with a very unusual style. He was called the "creator of devils" because he populated his pictures with creatures who symbolized man's struggle with evil. His masterpiece is a work called the *Garden of Earthly Delights*, which depicts the creation of woman in the left panel, the dreamlike centre where the figures are engaged in pleasure seeking, and the nightmare of Hell on the right, where those pleasures are being paid for throughout eternity.

Hieronymus Bosch, the right-hand panel from *The Garden of Earthly Delights*, 1510–15

Hugo van der Goes, *The Portinari Altarpiece*, 1476

86 The Renaissance

Painting | **The Arts in the Renaissance**

Renaissance painting in Northern Europe

Pieter Bruegel the Elder was the greatest Flemish painter of the 1500s. He is renowned for his landscapes and scenes of peasant life. He rejected the idealized figures of the Italian Renaissance in favour of realistic people in believable settings. His sons Jan and Pieter the Younger were also well-known artists.

Albrecht Dürer was a German painter and printmaker much influenced by the Italian Renaissance. He wanted to combine Italian theory with the native Northern interest in naturalistic detail. Dürer is perhaps best known for his woodcuts and engravings, which had a profound influence on German art in the 1500s.

Pieter Bruegel the Elder, *Peasant Wedding*, 1565

Pieter Bruegel the Elder, *The Return of the Hunters*, 1565

Albrecht Dürer, *The Four Horsemen of the Apocalypse*, 1523-26

Albrecht Dürer, self-portrait

Surely one of the most arrogant self-portraits ever: Dürer seems to be portraying himself as a Christ figure.

Albrecht Dürer, *Knight, Death and Devil*, 1523-26

The knight and the dog symbolize virtue, unafraid of the horseman of death in front or the devil behind.

The Renaissance

Musical Life in the Renaissance

Patrons

The main patrons of music in the Renaissance remained, as they were in the Middle Ages, the Church and the courts. The Church still needed music for all its public activities. Kings and queens, like Henry VIII and Elizabeth I in England and Francis I in France, were still important patrons. However, the demand for secular music increased with the rise of the city states, particularly in northern Italy. Aristocrats like the Medici in Florence wanted music to reflect their wealth and taste, and city fathers wanted music for civic rituals and ceremonies. So opportunities increased: musicians could be employed as composers and performers, choirmasters and builders of instruments for a greater range of clients.

The life of the musician

Most musicians began as choirboys in a church or in the chapel of an important court. The boys sang the soprano and alto parts, were taught music and some other subjects, and usually learned to play an instrument. When their voices changed, some would continue singing bass and tenor, and if they showed talent, be taught composition. The very best composers might then be hired as maestros di capella, or music directors. Once their reputations were made, composers could move to other, better positions, finding increasingly important patrons.

It is interesting that although the Renaissance was essentially an Italian creation, there were very few important Italian composers until Palestrina in the latter half of the sixteenth century. The major musicians of the period came from Flanders, the Netherlands and Burgundy, which is now part of France, and they travelled all over Europe as their services were required by the aristocratic courts.

Henry VIII was known to be a good musician. He also composed motets and love songs.

This painting shows the entertainment at a marriage celebration. You can see two different musical ensembles, as well as the dancers in the masque.

A group of musicians playing at a wedding

Choir boys singing

Professional Musicians | Musical Life in the Renaissance

Women musicians

Very few women were professional musicians during the Renaissance. When they did occur, they tended to be singers or perhaps instrumentalists. Nuns in convents regularly sang and there is some research to suggest that they composed as well. At the end of the sixteenth century, the convent of San Vito in Ferrara was particularly well-known for the quality of its music. The nuns there formed an ensemble, which was unusual in particular because it included instrumentalists as well as singers.

There was a professional group of four sopranos in Ferrara in the 1580s called the "Concerto della donne," or the "Ladies' Ensemble," who sang for the duke and duchess and their guests. They were very popular, and many composers wrote music for them that featured their high voices, adding an accompaniment for a bass instrument and harpsichord or lute. Imitators of the group appeared at other ducal courts in Italy. The existence of these groups of trained female singers undoubtedly had an effect on the appearance of roles for women in the new genre of opera, which emerged in the Baroque period.

Rarely were women given the opportunity to compose. One of the few recognized woman composers was Maddalena Casulana (c. 1544-90). A lutenist and singer as well, Casulana wrote three books of madrigals, and was the first woman to have her music published.

There were, of course, plenty of amateur women musicians. Music was an important skill and well-to-do women were encouraged to develop any talent they had on a social level. There were also women who influenced music from their positions as patrons of the arts.

This painting of women singing was done in sixteenth-century Venice.

Music in the home was increasingly important. These three young ladies are playing a song from a book of printed music, with one playing flute, another singing and a third on the lute. You can see the lute case hanging on the wall behind them.

The Renaissance 89

Musical Life in the Renaissance

Amateur Musicians

The rise in musical literacy

As more and more people in the upper and even merchant classes began to be educated, the ability to read music, sing, and play an instrument became an important social accomplishment. Well-to-do homes usually had a lute or a keyboard instrument, and musical training was part of a child's upbringing. Amateur musicians entertained themselves, playing chamber music or singing polyphonic songs. Early in the sixteenth century, a method for printing music was developed and printed music books became available, increasing the amount of music available for home performance and adding further impetus to the movement towards musical literacy.

This picture shows four well-to-do singers performing from printed part books.

Giovanni Petrucci of Venice used moveable type for printing music in the early 1500s. The best results occurred with a triple printing: first the staff was printed, then the notes, and finally the words were added.

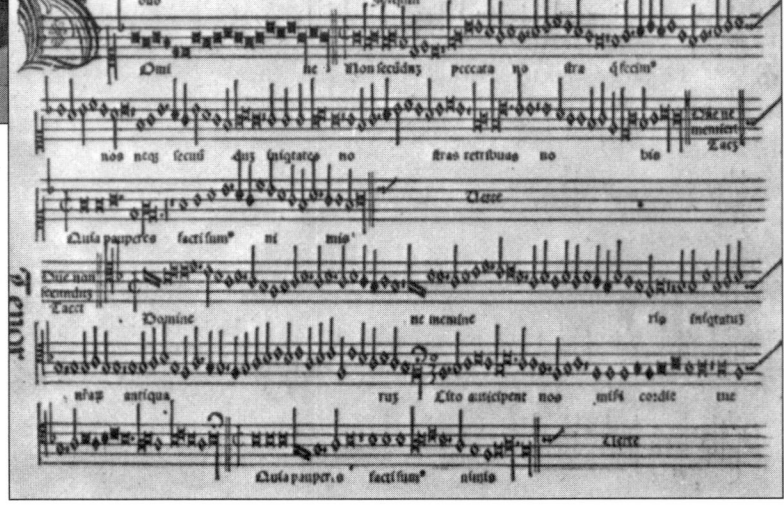

This domestic scene shows a young girl playing a cittern and gentleman accompanying her on the lute.

90 The Renaissance

General Features | **Characteristics of Renaissance Music**

Musical borrowing

Renaissance composers borrowed frequently from music that had already been written. This was not then considered cheating—originality in music is a modern concept—but an indication of esteem. They made use of existing plainsong melodies, well-known songs, and their own and other composer's works.

Modern melodies

In the Renaissance, composers liked to take the melodies from plainsong chants and highlight them, instead of using them as a foundation upon which to build their polyphonic structures. They added notes, made the rhythms more fluid and generally "updated" them to their taste. This process was called paraphrase. You can see in the example below how the composer has used all the notes in the chant melody but changed their duration and added more notes for a fuller, richer sound. In addition, the melody is no longer at the bottom, but given to the soprano voice.

The bottom two staves show the beginning of Josquin Desprez's Kyrie *from the* Missa Pange Lingua. *The top one shows the original chant melody.*

This illustration shows the process of paraphrasing. The dotted lines indicate the notes taken directly from the plainsong.

Expression

Renaissance composers, as people living in an era of humanist thought, were aware of the musical ideas of antiquity, and knew that ancient philosophers believed that music could arouse emotion. They knew that poets could express emotion with words, and they sought to do the same thing indirectly by illustrating the words in their texts musically. Renaissance composers had a much greater sensitivity to the words in the texts they were using than did composers of the Middle Ages.

Music in the Renaissance 91

Characteristics of Renaissance Music

Specific Features

Imitation

The technique of imitation involved having each voice in the music present the same musical phrase successively; each line enters one after the other, so the listener has the sense that the music overlaps. Everyone is familiar with singing canons, or rounds, like *Frère Jacques*—this is imitation in its strictest form, where each voice sings exactly the same thing. But Renaissance composers also used a freer imitation, in which only the first few notes of a melody are repeated by each voice, which then continues with its own polyphonic line. Imitation made Renaissance music sound smoother and more harmonious, with less contrast between each voice than had been the case in the Middle Ages.

The upper staves illustrate strict imitation (a round); the lower ones, free imitation.

A section from Palestrina's *Missa brevis* showing the technique of imitation. In this section, the voices enter in ascending order.

Music in the Renaissance

Harmony

Renaissance composers developed new ideas about consonance. In the late Middle Ages, European musicians tended to regard only fourths, fifths and octaves as consonances. In England, however, the intervals of the third and the sixth were in common use, and under the influence of the English composer John Dunstable who was present in the Burgundian court in the early fifteenth century, the third and the sixth became acceptable consonances across Europe. At this same time, composers seemed to be developing a sense of tonality, the concept that a work begins with a definite keynote and returns to it again at the end. They were also beginning to think of harmony as vertical, concerning themselves with the notes that occurred at the same time in all the voices, rather than only thinking in a linear way of the melodies that fit together in the counterpoint. By the end of the sixteenth century, writing in counterpoint lost its sway and composers often put more emphasis on one melodic line supported by chords. The bass line supported all the harmonies above, often written with figures below the notes to indicate the chords. This was the beginning of the figured bass, or basso continuo, so prominent in the Baroque period. This concept of the melody and the bass lines being the important ones with the parts in the middle being harmonic fill is very different from the polyphonic view, which saw all voices as equally important. In addition, composers were gradually working outside the ancient Church modes, adding additional notes that broke down the distinction between the modes. This would lead gradually to a reduction in the number of modes to just major and minor, and the end of the modal system. It opened the way to the supremacy of tonality.

Each of the voices here is stacked vertically with each note being of exactly the same duration.

In this fragment, we see that the composer has used the middle line to indicate the harmonies he wants the keyboard player to fill in.

| Characteristics of Renaissance Music | Specific Features |

Treatment of words

Because the words they were setting to music were so important, Renaissance composers developed new ways of emphasizing their significance. First of all, they began to write music that conformed to the normal rhythms of speech so that the words fit naturally and beautifully with the melodies. This is not true of mediaeval music, in which the structure of the music was much more important than the words. Secondly, they developed the technique of word painting, in which the music was matched to the meaning of the word. Words like "flying" or "heaven" were accompanied by rising notes, "happiness" by sweet-sounding chords, "death," "torment" and "grief" by discordant ones. A "sigh" could be signified by a rest, or a falling two-pitch figure. When used sensitively, this technique added a great deal to the emotional expressiveness of the music, and it has been used by composers in all later periods.

The architecture of St. Mark's Cathedral made antiphonal singing possible.

Polychoral music

Venice was a major Italian musical centre during the Renaissance, with a series of strong choirmasters and organists. Particularly common there was the use of antiphonal choirs, two or three choirs who answered each other alternately as well as singing together. This made echo effects possible as one choir responded to another. The St. Mark's cathedral, the most famous church in Venice, had two organs installed. The choirmaster would have a choir at each organ and others placed around the church, producing a kind of "surround-sound" effect.

| Music in the Renaissance |

Liturgical Forms   Characteristics of Renaissance Music

The mass

By the end of the Middle Ages, composers were primarily writing polyphonic music for the main parts of the mass. The five parts of the mass that are sung every day—the *Kyrie, Gloria, Credo, Sanctus*, and *Agnus Dei*— are called the Ordinary, and it was on these five sections that Renaissance composers concentrated their efforts. They wanted to make the music of the mass more of an organic whole even though they were separated during the service. One of the ways they did this was to base them all on the same original source, called the *cantus firmus*, often a plainchant melody or a popular song. Usually the source is most obvious in the tenor voice, but it often appears in the other voices as well. Another unifying aspect of the music was the use of imitation. Composers also tied everything together by using a similar opening for all five sections. Another type of mass was the parody mass, in which the musical material is taken from previously written motets, chansons or madrigals. The pre-existing work was usually broken into fragments and used in different places in the mass, surrounded by new material.

La Messe de saint Grégoire, unknown French painter, fifteenth century

The opening section of the mass, the *Kyrie*, is a prayer for mercy. Its language is Greek, as opposed to the Latin of the rest of the mass, and its form is ABA: three repetitions of *Kyrie eleison* (Lord have mercy), three of *Christe eleison* (Christ have mercy) and a final three of *Kyrie eleison*. The second section is the *Gloria* (Glory to God in the highest), and the third is the *Credo* (I believe in one God, the Father Almighty), the Christian's statement of faith. The fourth part is the *Sanctus* (Holy, holy, holy) ending with the Hosanna (Hosanna in the highest) and the Benedictus (Blessed is he who comes in the name of the Lord). The last section, the *Agnus Dei* (Lamb of God, who takes away the sins of the world), ends with the words *Dona nobis pacem*—give us peace. This five-section form of the mass was solidified during the Renaissance and is still standard in Roman Catholic churches today.

An illuminated manuscript showing a *Kyrie*

This mass is being celebrated with a choir and an instrumental ensemble.

Music in the Renaissance

Characteristics of Renaissance Music

Liturgical Forms

The motet

Another important form of liturgical music in the Renaissance was the motet, although its form had little in common with the motets written in the Middle Ages by composers like Pérotin and Machaut. Renaissance motet is a short setting of a Latin text consisting of smaller sections written in a mixture of homophony (melody supported by chords) and imitative polyphony. The words are religious, often from the Bible, and they offered composers more flexibility than the mass, in which the words are invariable. They could choose texts that expressed the dramatic or mysterious aspects of religion, which offered the opportunity for richer, more expressive music. Often motets were written in honour of the Virgin Mary. Renaissance motet is a vocal work entirely, sung in four parts by a small choir. One of the most important composers of the Renaissance motet was Josquin Desprez (1440-1521). He was of the Franco-Flemish school and completed the transformation from the Middle Ages to the Renaissance.

Lucas Cranach, *Martin Luther*

Luther was a fine singer and played the flute and the lute.

New forms

New musical forms for use in the Church service appeared with the Reformation. The Lutheran Church in Germany introduced the chorale, with the entire congregation singing unaccompanied in unison. The texts were often translations from Latin plainsong texts set to simple secular song melodies. Subsequently, harmony was created with the addition of a choir, or instrumental accompaniment, like an organ. Until about 1700, none of the other Protestant Churches allowed hymns without biblical texts, and their congregational music was primarily based on texts from the Book of Psalms. In England, the Anglican Church developed the anthem, the counterpart of the Roman Catholic motet.

Ein' fe - ste Burg ist un - ser Gott

The first few bars of Luther's most famous chorale, *Ein Feste Burg* (*A Mighty Fortress*)

Secular Forms | Characteristics of Renaissance Music

The chanson

The chanson was a great favourite at the court of the dukes of Burgundy, who were important patrons of the arts in the early Renaissance. Chansons were written for three voices, with either or both lower voices being instrumental. The texts used were the courtly love poems of the French Renaissance, and the forms followed the poetic structure. If there were repeated sections in the text, this was also the case with music. The poetic forms used were the rondeau, the ballad and the virelay. By the end of the fifteenth century, a new style of chanson was being written. Flemish composer Josquin Desprez moved to four voices singing the same text, sometimes using a melody-with-chord structure, in others using imitation. In the sixteenth century, fifth and sixth voices were added.

A flutist and a lutenist playing a polyphonic chanson

This collection of love songs and ballads is called *Le Chansonnier de Tournai*.

A line of musicians and spectators separates two songs in a manuscript of *La Bataille de Marignan* by Clément Janequin.

Music in the Renaissance

Characteristics of Renaissance Music

Secular Forms

The madrigal

Another type of secular song, the madrigal, developed in Italy, although it ultimately flourished in several European countries. Madrigals originated in the fourteenth century, then went into a decline and re-emerged in the sixteenth. One important predecessor of the madrigal was the frottola, a song with instrumental accompaniment, generally a soprano or alto melody and two harmonizing parts below. Later frottolas were written with four voices, each provided with text, perhaps doubled by instruments as well, preparing the way for the four-voiced madrigal.

The sixteenth-century madrigal is a vocal piece for a small group of singers, perhaps just one per part, set to the text of a short poem, usually five to fourteen lines, with the last two lines being a rhyming couplet. The favourite topics were love and nature, but they also dealt with humour, political satire and portrayals of city and country life. The musical techniques were homophony and imitative polyphony, as in liturgical music, but madrigal composers worked even harder to express the meaning of the words directly in the music. Developing contrasts between the different emotions aroused by the music was a measure of the composer's skill.

A young Claudio Monteverdi

The earlier Italian madrigals were primarily written for the enjoyment of the performers, but as the form developed, composers increasingly sought to impress their audiences with the virtuosity of the singers and their own expressivity. The best known composers of Italian madrigals were Flemish composers working in Italy, like Adriaan Willaert and Orlando di Lasso, and Italians like Palestrina and Andrea Gabrieli. The form lasted into the early decades of the Baroque period. One of the late masters was Claudio Monteverdi, who is perhaps best known as an early Baroque opera composer.

The madrigal was particularly popular in England, and English composers like Thomas Morley, William Byrd and Orlando Gibbons adopted the Italian madrigal as English poets had adopted the Italian sonnet. Sometimes they translated from the Italian—in 1590, a group of madrigals was published under the title *Italian Madrigals Englished*—but they also wrote their own madrigals with English texts. Often these were lighter and more cheerful than the Italian madrigals.

Music in the Renaissance

Instrumental Music | **Characteristics of Renaissance Music**

Composing for instruments

During the Middle Ages, instruments were mainly used to double or substitute for vocal parts in a work, or to provide dance music. In the Renaissance, however, composers began to write music to showcase instrumentalists and their talents. By the late Renaissance, works were being written for specific instruments that took into account their capabilities and limitations.

Instrumental music in the Renaissance was written for four main instruments or groups: the lute, the organ, stringed keyboard instruments and instrumental ensembles. The lute was an extremely popular instrument. It was tuned much like the guitar, but it had double strings. The soundbox was half-spherical and the finger board angled back from the flat side of the body. The organ, because of its involvement with liturgical music, was a very important instrument. Other keyboard instruments included the harpsichord, virginals, and spinet, which were sounded with a plucked string, and the clavichord, whose strings were struck by a metal tongue, or tangent.

Instrumental ensembles incorporated various combinations of available instruments: viols, woodwinds and brasses. Viols come from a different family of instruments than the modern violin. They have sloped shoulders and frets on the finger board, and a much softer sound. Most common was the viola da gamba, or "leg viol" which was held in the lap or between the legs like a modern cello. They came in soprano, alto, tenor and bass sizes. There were also viola da braccias, or "arm viols," which were played like a violin. Renaissance woodwinds included the recorder, and the transverse flute, played sideways, like the modern flute. There was also the shawm, a double-reeded instrument that is the ancestor of the oboe. The krummhorn was another double-reeded instrument with a nasal buzzing sound. Available brass instruments were the sackbut, an early trombone, and the trumpet, which was not very popular. There was also the cornetto, which was kind of a hybrid; it had a trumpet-like mouthpiece but was made of wood with holes in its body and covered in leather. It sounded rather like a soft trumpet.

At first the violin was seen as a kind of "country cousin" to the viol, unfit for sophisticated performances and reserved for peasant dance forms. Only in France was it prized, and there it replaced the more awkward viol.

This picture shows a group of instrumentalists that includes two singers, a flute player, a violist, a lutenist and someone playing a portative organ.

This ensemble includes outdoor instruments, like the crumhorn, pipe and tabor and shawms.

Music in the Renaissance 99

Characteristics of Renaissance Music

Instrumental Forms

Dance forms

Renaissance dance forms were generally composed in pairs as they had been in the Middle Ages, although sometimes composers wrote sets of three or more, suggesting the beginnings of the dance suites of the Baroque period. The dance pairs were usually contrasting in tempo and metre, but linked by the same melody. The slow and stately pavane in duple metre was followed by the vigorous galliard, in triple metre, which had four hopping steps and a leap that the men took higher than the women. Another common pair were the allemande and the courante, the former being a slow, flowing dance, and the latter faster, with running steps. With the advent of music publishing, collections of dance music were available both for solo instruments and ensembles.

Jean Patin, The Duc de Joyeuse's Ball

Keyboard forms

Organs differed from other keyboard instruments of the period in that the organ was able to produce a sustained note for as long as the organist held the key down and there was wind in the bellows. So Renaissance organ music shows a combination of long notes and chords plus the same rapid passages and trills and different ornamentations that the other keyboard instruments could play. Preludes were works that were played as an introduction to a larger composition, and they were very popular for organ, as were fantasias and toccatas. The latter are sometimes hard to tell apart, but the toccata is characterized by sections of rapid, showy passages designed to illustrate the performer's technique.

Other forms

The ricercare, written for various instruments ranging from organ to lute, has several themes which the composer develops through imitation. The name is applied to a variety of pieces, but the classic sixteenth-century ricercare was like a motet, with several sections, each using imitation. The canzona was derived from the French vocal chanson, alternating between polyphonic and chordal sections. It almost always began with the same rhythmic pattern, a half note followed by two quarter notes. Instrumental canzonas developed in the late sixteenth century. The keyboard canzona was highly polyphonic and is regarded as a precursor to the Baroque fugue; the instrumental canzona featured contrasting tempos and rhythms and is seen as the ancestor of the Baroque trio sonata.

Les Anges musiciens, by Hubert and Jan van Eyck, shows an angel at the keyboard of a portative organ.

Music in the Renaissance

Early Renaissance | Composers

The Burgundian school

Throughout the first half of the fifteenth century, the successive courts of the Dukes of Burgundy were known for the brilliance of their music. At the time, the dukes were powerful rivals of the kings of France and allies of the English, ruling over a territory that covered most of eastern France and the Low Countries (Belgium, Luxembourg and the Netherlands). They attracted the leading musicians of the day. The most significant of these was **Guillaume Dufay (c. 1400-74)**. Dufay was born in Cambrai, France, and trained in Italy, including two periods with the papal choir. In addition to the dukes of Burgundy, his patrons included the dukes of Ferrara and Savoy. He maintained a connection with Cambrai, and lived and worked there for the last sixteen years of his life.

This illustration shows Dufay with a portative organ and Binchois with a harp.

In many ways Dufay's music is a fusion of late mediaeval French music with the early Renaissance style from Italy. Dufay seems to reject the complicated style of the previous era in favour of clear melodies and sharply defined rhythms. He is said to have introduced the fauxbourdon technique to written music. Fauxbourdon is a musical texture made up of three voices, a plainchant melody with the lowest voice running in parallel motion a sixth below, and a middle, unwritten part at a fourth below the top note, creating in essence an inverted triad, which produces a very consonant sound. In his later career, he is also noted for expanding the standard number of voices in a musical work to four. He wrote all kinds of music, secular and liturgical, including many chansons and motets, and at least nine complete masses. His mass settings are for four voices and use a *cantus firmus* taken from plainchant or a popular melody in the tenor line, which he works into each section of the mass. He used the popular song *L'Homme armé* as the basis of one of his masses, and for another, his own ballad *Se la face ay pale*.

A contemporary of Dufay's was **Gilles Binchois (c. 1400-60)**, who served Philip the Good of Burgundy for 30 years. Binchois is particularly known for his mastery of the secular chanson. Burgundy's alliance with England explains the influence of the English composer **John Dunstable (c. 1385-1453)** on Dufay and Binchois. Dunstable was in the service of the Duke of Bedford, who was the military opponent of Joan of Arc. The harmonies in Dunstable's masses, motets and secular songs were in the English tradition, more consonant, full of sonorous thirds and sixths.

Gilles Binchois

Music in the Renaissance 101

Composers

Early Renaissance

The Franco-Flemish school

The Franco-Flemish school was the style of music that dominated European music in the last half of the fifteenth century. It was called that because the most important musicians came from northern France, Flanders or the Netherlands. These musicians travelled all over Europe and served in many royal courts, including the Medici in Florence and the Sforza in Milan. Most significant were Johannes Ockeghem, Jacob Obrecht, Clément Janequin and especially, Josquin Desprez.

Johannes Ockeghem (c. 1410-97) was Flemish. He first appeared in musical records as a singer in the Antwerp Cathedral; he served as composer to three French kings, and was made treasurer of the abbey of Saint-Martin at Tours, where he died at the age of about 87. Ockeghem is important for his work with the cyclic mass, based on the concept that the different parts of the Ordinary should be pulled together with the use of one melody or chant. He was a master of the canon technique, a form of imitation in which a melody is imitated strictly in one or more other parts at different time intervals. In his *Missa prolationum*, he uses two two-part canons at different rates of speed. Ockeghem's compositional style for his masses was different from that of his secular music. They were more solemn, usually written in four voices and with longer melodic lines. His three-voice chansons make greater use of melodic imitation and have simpler rhythms. He left 14 masses, 10 motets and 20 chansons.

This manuscript illumination shows Ockeghem leading a group of singers.

Jacob Obrecht (1452-1505) was born in Bergen-op-Zoom, Brabant, now a part of the Netherlands. He is known to have worked at Cambrai Cathedral in France, the cathedral at Bruges in Flanders, and at the court of the Duke of Ferrara, where he died of the plague in 1505. Obrecht's surviving works include 27 masses, 19 motets and 31 secular pieces. Most of his masses are for four voices using a *cantus firmus*, usually in the tenor voice, but sometimes in the other voices as well. The motets are generally celebrations of the Virgin Mary, such as *Salve Regina* and *Alma Redemptoris Mater*.

Music in the Renaissance

Early Renaissance | **Composers**

The Franco-Flemish school

Josquin Desprez (c. 1485-1521) is the most significant composer of the Franco-Flemish school. He was born in Hainaut, near the present day border of France and Belgium. He served the Sforza family in Milan for about ten years, and then went to the papal chapel in Rome. He worked for Louis XII of France and the Duke of Ferrara, before returning to Condé-sur-Escaut in his native region to be the provost of Notre-Dame church for the last sixteen years of his life. His peers considered him the greatest musician of his period, combining technical ingenuity with the ability to express emotion.

Manuscript showing a four-part section of the Pane Lingua *Mass*

Josquin is best known for his choral liturgical works, his main contribution being his development of the motet. He used a four-voice imitation technique in which each voice enters singing in imitation a modified version of the pre-existing chant melody. After all have entered, there is a free section where the musical elements become more elaborate. This increases tension, which is released with a cadence. Josquin's cadences are called overlapped, because the next section of entries in one voice is begun as the other three voices sing the last note of the current cadence. This technique of four-voice imitation in which the melodies for each voice are based on the pre-existing melody is called "motet style."

Josquin Desprez

He left 20 masses and more than 100 motets as well as a number of chansons. Among Josquin's masses are the *Missa l'Homme Armé Sexti Toni* (*Sixth Tone Mass on L'Homme armé*), and the *Missa Malheur me bat*. The *Missa Pange Lingua*, considered one of his masterpieces, is written in motet style.

Clément Janequin (c. 1485-1558) was the leading sixteenth-century French chanson composer. He wrote 286 chansons, the best known of which are program chansons like "La Bataille de Marignan," which features battle sounds, "Voulez ouïr les cris de Paris," imitating the cries of street vendors in Paris, and "Le Chant des oiseaux" with bird songs. He was one of the few composers who never had a regular, important post with an aristocrat or prince of the Church.

A page from Josquin's manuscript of Déploration de Guillaume Crétin sur le trépas de Johannes Ockeghem, *an elegy written on the death of Ockeghem*

Music in the Renaissance

Composers

High Renaissance

Giovanni Pierluigi da Palestrina

Palestrina

Giovanni Pierluigi da Palestrina (1525-94), called Palestrina after the town where he was born, spent most of his life composing music for three of the great Roman churches. When the Bishop of Palestrina was elected as Pope Julius III in 1550, Palestrina was made music director for the Julian Chapel choir and therefore in charge of the music at St. Peter's Basilica. He lost this position when the next pope refused to allow married men in the choir. He spent sixteen years as music director at two other important churches in Rome, before returning to his old position at St. Peter's. He was later given the title of master of music at the Vatican Basilica. Palestrina considered entering the priesthood when his wife and two elder sons died in the plague epidemic of 1580, but instead married a wealthy widow a year later. Pope Gregory XIII asked Palestrina to restore the plainsong then in use in the church to a more authentic style, but he never completed this monumental task. He remained at his post as music director of the Julian Chapel choir, in spite of several attempts to lure him away, and published a great deal of music in the last years of his life.

Palestrina was a prolific composer, writing more than 100 masses and about 400 motets, of which 250 remain. His style is noted for its balance, purity, control and clarity and its emphasis on the integrity of the texts. He achieved this in two ways. First was the control of the melodic line in his works so that the movement was essentially in small steps with very few leaps, and any leaps that do occur are balanced by movement in the opposite direction. Second was his control over dissonance. He makes use of dissonance, but the dissonant notes are usually of short duration or off the beat, and immediately resolved. He balanced polyphony and harmony in his works so that the words were particularly clear and in a natural rhythm. His masses were written in many different styles. Some used a traditional *cantus firmus* in the tenor line, others were based on the canon technique, still others on parody technique, using fragments of already exiting music. He also wrote a number of masses in free style, in which all the musical ideas were entirely original. Perhaps his most famous mass is the *Pope Marcellus* mass, written for six voices and performed *a capella*, without accompaniment. Six voices were quite typical for the all-male church choirs of the time. The highest voice was sung by boy sopranos, the alto by male altos or countertenors, with two tenor and two bass lines. Palestrina's motets are nearly as varied as his masses. The 29 motets based on the biblical texts from the *Song of Solomon* incorporate many madrigal techniques.

An engraving used as the title page of Palestrina's first book of masses showing the composer presenting a printed copy of his work to Pope Julian III

High Renaissance | Composers

Orlando di Lasso

Orlando di Lassso (c. 1530-94) was a Flemish composer who went to Italy at the age of 12 or 14, working at several courts until he was appointed music director at the important church of St. John Lateran in Rome at the age of 21. From there he moved to Munich, where he was in charge of the chapel for the Duke of Bavaria until his death. Lasso wrote over 2 000 works, most of which were published during his lifetime. Many were sacred motets and madrigals, but he also wrote secular music in several international styles. His chansons in the French style were often based on the poetry of Pierre de Ronsard and Clément Marot, but he also wrote German lieder and drinking songs, as well as delicate Italian madrigals. His best known work may be a collection of psalm settings called *Psalmi Davidis Poenitentiales*.

Orlando di Lasso

Tomas Luis de Victoria

Born in Spain, **Tomas Luis de Victoria (c. 1548-1611)** ranks with Palestrina and di Lasso in significance, although he has many fewer works to his credit. Victoria studied in Rome, perhaps with Palestrina, and then worked there for a time. When he was 30, he became chaplain to the dowager empress Maria, widow of Maximilian II, the Holy Roman Emperor. When she entered a convent in Madrid, Victoria went with her as her priest and organist and remained there until his death. Victoria wrote liturgical music almost exclusively. His compositions include 21 masses and 44 motets as well as some psalm settings, hymns, and several Magnificats. He brought intense dramatic feeling to his music, a certain Spanish mysticism, and his harmonies were more chromatic than those of his contemporaries. He was a master of imitation and the reworking of existing musical material. His choral works were accompanied by instruments doubling the vocal parts, and the organ parts foreshadow the Baroque continuo.

Orlando di Lasso at the harpsichord conducting the musicians of the chapel of the Duke of Bavaria

Orlando di Lasso's choir at the Bavarian Court Chapel

Music in the Renaissance   105

Andrea and Giovanni Gabrieli

Andrea Gabrieli (c. 1510-86) and his nephew **Giovanni** (c. 1556-1612) were the pre-eminent composers in Venice. Both were organists at St. Mark's Cathedral there. The cathedral's architecture and acoustics suggested certain possibilities to Andrea and he sometimes divided up his choirs and instrumentalists so that the people in the audience would hear the music coming from different directions. He is best known for the large choral and instrumental works he wrote for ceremonial occasions, although he also was an active madrigalist. Giovanni Gabrieli studied under his uncle and accompanied him on foreign travels, which undoubtedly helped the younger man to achieve a reputation abroad. Giovanni also studied under Orlando di Lasso in Munich. Giovanni developed the concept of multiple choirs to the full. Working with so many singers caused him to move away from polyphony and towards a homophonic style; having all the singers singing the same word at the same time made the words much clearer. Giovanni was one of the first composers to add dynamic markings to his scores, and he often specified the make-up of the choirs and which instruments were to be used, exploring the possibilities of balance between voice and instruments. His emphasis on dynamic contrast, particularly in his *Sonata pian' e forte* for strings and wind instruments, and his development of the concerto-type style is a bridge to the Baroque period.

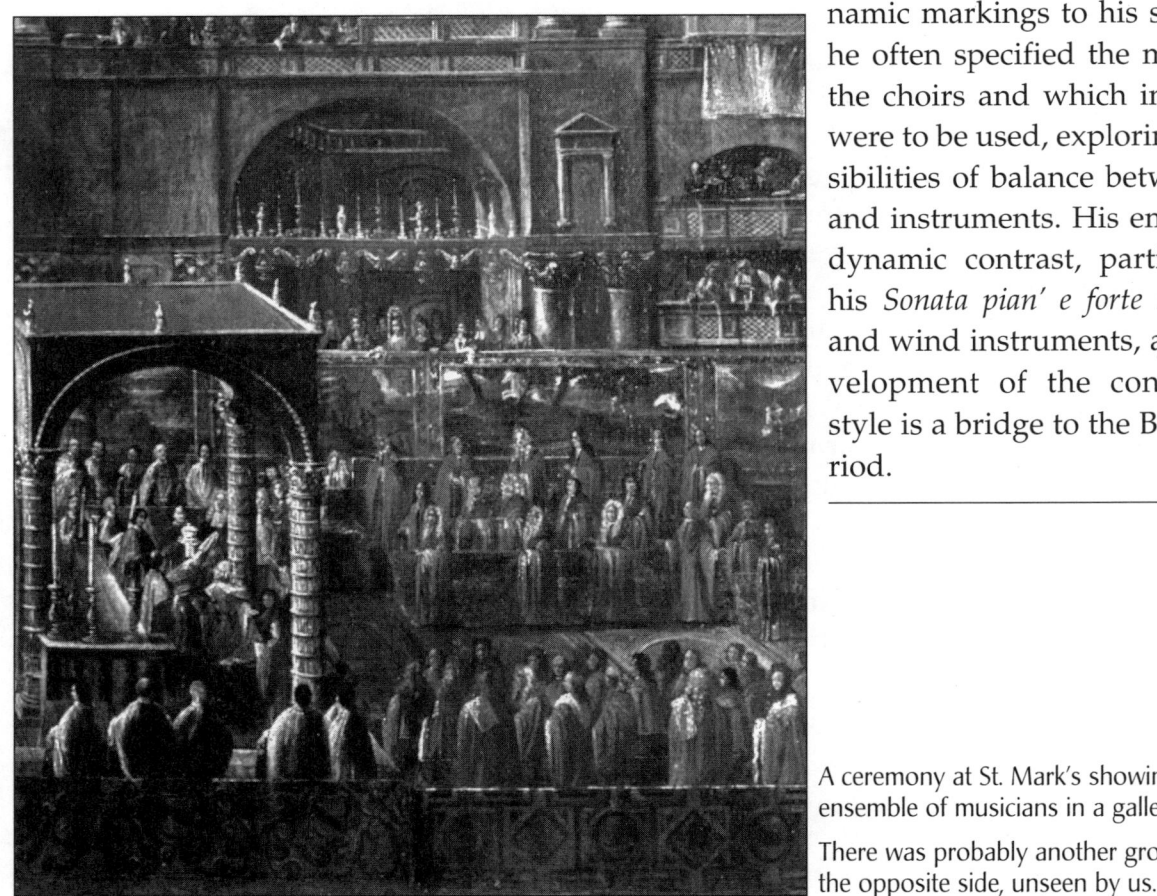

A ceremony at St. Mark's showing one ensemble of musicians in a gallery

There was probably another group on the opposite side, unseen by us.

High Renaissance

Composers

The English school

Thomas Tallis (c. 1510-85) is perhaps the most important composer of English sacred music of the first half of the sixteenth century, responsible for introducing European style polyphony to England. He served Henry VIII, Edward VI, Mary Tudor and Elizabeth I as an organist in the Chapel Royal, and his career spans the transition in England from Catholicism to Protestantism. His surviving works in Latin include three masses, two Magnificats, two Lamentations and 52 motets. Two of these works in particular demonstrate Tallis's command of polyphonic technique, the motet *Spem in alium*, written for 40 voices, and the seven-part *Miserere nostri*, a canonic masterpiece. He was one of the first composers to set words to music for the Anglican service, as well as writing over 20 anthems and three sets of psalms. He also left 23 keyboard pieces.

William Byrd (1543-1623) is the greatest English composer of the latter half of the sixteenth century. He was a protégé of Tallis, and shared the post as organist for the Chapel Royal with Tallis for a few years. The two men were granted a monopoly for printing music and music paper by Queen Elizabeth. Byrd was raised a Catholic under the regime of Mary Tudor, but he does not seem to have been persecuted for his religion when Protestantism returned under Elizabeth. He wrote music for both Churches, including three Latin masses and many motets, the best known of which is *Ave verum corpus*. He also wrote two complete Anglican services, and more than 20 anthems with organ or other instrumental accompaniment. Byrd is also noted as a composer of keyboard works, both for solo instruments and ensembles. His many pieces for the virginal set the standard for later English composers. Many are dance movements in which he illustrates his skill with variations. He also wrote four Fantasias in three to six parts for viol consort and secular vocal music for voice and viol consort.

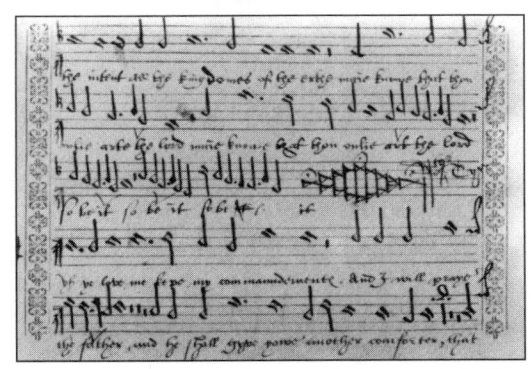

Thomas Tallis

William Byrd

A manuscript of a piece of Tallis's church music

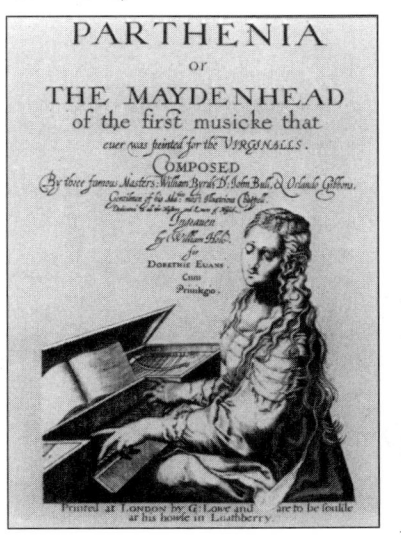

The title page from the first book of keyboard music to be published in England. It contains pairs of dances by William Byrd and Orlando Gibbons.

Music in the Renaissance

Composers

High Renaissance

The English school

Thomas Morley (c. 1557-1602), a composer, organist and theoretician, was the first of the English madrigalists. A pupil of Byrd, he was an organist at St. Paul's and later at the Chapel Royal. He also inherited Byrd and Tallis's monopoly on music printing in England. Morley was trained in Byrd's polyphonic tradition, but he became interested in the possibilities offered by the Italian madrigal set to English texts. He wrote two collections of canzonets (which he called "little short songs") and then began composing and publishing madrigals. His madrigal style shows clarity of texture, sprightly rhythms and warm harmonies. His *Plaine and Easie Introduction to Practicall Musicke* was the most celebrated English music theory book of the period.

As well as being a composer, **John Dowland (c. 1562-1626)** was also a singer and virtuoso on the lute. He spent a number of years on the continent and brought back many new ideas. He was the outstanding composer of the ayre, a form of solo song with lute or instrumental consort accompaniment that was particularly popular in England in the late sixteenth century. Many ayres resemble dance music, and they often have the same music for each stanza.

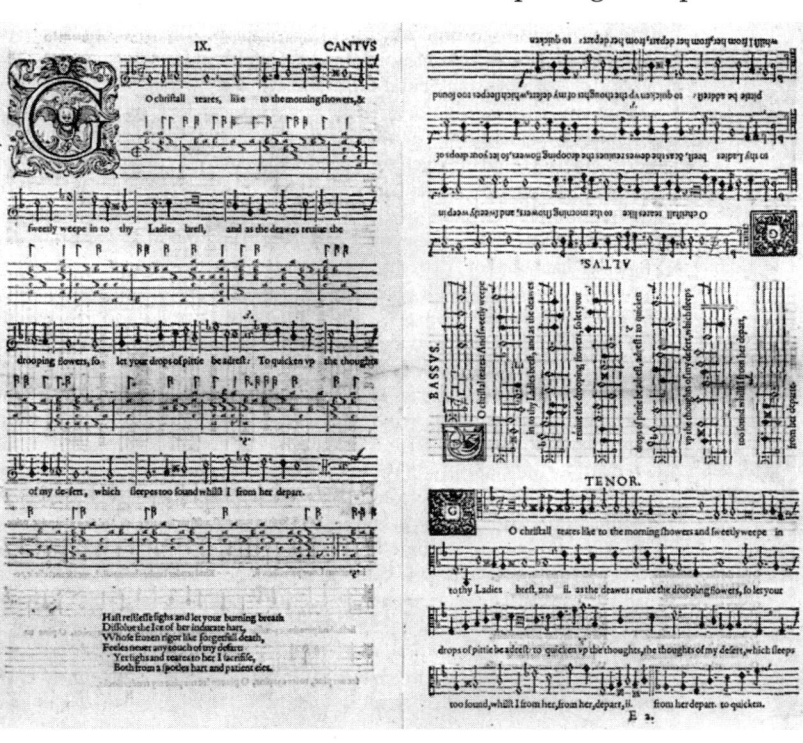

"Go christall tears" from Dowland's *First Book of Songs or Ayres*

This song is printed so that in addition to the solo voice and lute version on the left, three additional voice parts are found on the other side so that four singers sitting around a table could read it.

Orlando Gibbons (1583-1625) is one of the last composers of the English Renaissance. He was made organist of the Chapel Royal at the age of 21, and he remained so for his lifetime. He was well-known for his church music, and his anthems are particularly distinguished. He is also acclaimed for his madrigals, particularly *The Silver Swanne* and *What is Our Life?*. He was an eminent organist and virginalist; many of his virginal pieces survive in manuscript form.

Orlando Gibbons

Printed in October 2000
Centre franco-ontarien de ressources pédagogiques

Art Gallery
The Middle Ages

8

9

10

11

12

Political Situation | **Life in the Middle Ages**

In the early Middle Ages, the Franks were one of the first groups to make themselves into something like a state. Name their leader, who is considered to be the first King of France: _____

The Empire of the Franks reached its peak around 800 under a king who ruled over a huge territory that stretched across most of Europe. He was a strong believer in civilization and encouraged education. Give his name: _____

Between 800 and 1100, a group of ferocious warriors from Scandinavia raided the shores of Europe and the British Isles. What is the name of these invaders? _____

In 1066, a Norman warrior crossed the channel to England, killed the Saxon King Harold at the Battle of Hastings and claimed the crown of England. Give his name: _____

What was the main system of political organization in the Middle Ages? _____

Under this system, the society was divided into three distinct groups.
What were they? 1. _____ 2. _____ 3. _____

At the time, all the land was generally owned by the king. He divided the land into fiefs and granted portions of land to which privileged group of people? _____

Name the system that describes the relationship between the landowners and the people who worked the land: _____

Name two groups of men that were very powerful among the ranks of the clergy:
1. _____ 2. _____

By the beginning of the Middle Ages, the Christian religion had spread all around the Mediterranean area and throughout Europe. The Christian Church had a great deal of influence over the kings and rulers of the various groups. What is the name given to the head of that Church, now called the Roman Catholic Church, who normally resides in Rome? _____

One of the reasons for the powerful influence of the Church was the monasteries. They were responsible for preserving what written records were left of the previous Roman Empire and its culture.

Explain what is being shown in this illustration:
_____
_____
_____

Pilgrimages to the Holy Land were an important tradition for Christians. Responding to the call of Pope Urban II, nobles from all across Europe lead large armies into a holy war to recapture Jerusalem. Over a period of 200 years, seven major military expeditions were sent to attack the Muslims. These expeditions were called : _____

Life in the Middle Ages

Mediaeval thought

In the Middle Ages, thinkers were more interested in finding salvation after death through religion than in focussing on the investigation of nature and the search for human happiness. Name the Christian philosopher of the fourth century who thought that man needed both the Christian emphasis on faith and emotion and the Greek insistence on reason, and who had a profound influence on the Middle Ages:

_____

It is through the translations of Arab scholars that the works of Aristotle, Plato and other Greek philosophers came to the attention of theologians in Western Europe during the twelfth century. Name an important jurist and physician who was the most important Muslim philosopher of his time: _____

The doctrine of an important philosopher of the late mediaeval period became the accepted philosophy of the Roman Catholic Church, and continued to influence philosophers into the twentieth century. Name this philosopher and theologian: _____

Universities originated in the mediaeval period. Name the universities established in the twelfth and thirteenth centuries—all these universities are all still in operation today: _____
_____

Society and Culture

Mediaeval society was essentially organized around war. Match each illustration with one of the statements below:

1. 2. 3.

_____ Sons of the nobility would undertake a long apprenticeship to become a knight.

_____ In the early Middle Ages, tournaments were a way of training knights for battle. Later, they became a form of entertainment for the court and a way for knights to demonstrate their skills.

_____ The code of chivalry dictated how a knight should behave. The notion of courtly love associated with this code had an important impact on music. Knights were expected to write poetry, sing love songs and play musical instruments as a way of pleasing their lady.

Peasants were of two kinds. Identify each one and describe in a few words the work they did.

_____   _____
_____   _____
_____   _____
_____   _____
_____   _____

| Literature | The Arts in the Middle Ages |

Old English poetry was primarily designed to be chanted. Name the first epic poem, written down in the eighth century: _____

Name the first important work in English literature written in the fourteenth century and name the author: _____

Name the work that is a collection of stories written in the fifteenth century about King Arthur and the Knights of the Round Table, and name the author: _____
_____

What is the name given to the earliest works written in French, which were long poems about the exploits of Christian knights? _____

Name a famous poem written at the beginning of the twelfth century telling about the deeds of Roland, a knight at Charlemagne's court: _____

Name a famous French poet who wrote poems about chivalry and courtly love based on the legends surrounding the English King Arthur and his knights: _____

Name the 22,000-line poem describing love as a rosebud living in a garden, which symbolizes the life of chivalry: _____

Name the best-known fifteenth-century French poet: _____

Name the epic poem that is the oldest piece of literature written in German: _____

Many more German epic poems were written in the twelfth and thirteenth centuries. Name the most famous one upon which the nineteenth-century composer Richard Wagner based his opera cycle, *The Ring of the Nibelungen*: _____

Name one of the first Italian writers, who is still considered one of the greatest writers of all time:
_____

Name his masterpiece, an epic poem divided into three sections: _____

Name another important fourteenth-century Italian writer, who is seen as the first modern poet:
_____

Mediaeval theatre took different forms depending on its content and the place where it was performed. For each description below, name the type of play:

Type of play	miracle play	liturgical drama	morality play
	Scenes from the Bible, spoken in Latin, performed in the church and designed to teach religious lessons.		
	Scenes with more secular content, spoken in the local language and performed by the townspeople in the town market places.		
	Scenes with no biblical content usually performed by professional minstrels. The best-known English one is *Everyman*		

3

The Arts in the Middle Ages
Architecture, Sculpture, Painting and Decorative Arts

Architecture

In the Middle Ages, most of the major architectural works were built for the Church. In the Art Gallery, find an illustration that matches each description below.

_____ A Romanesque church with a stone-vaulted ceiling. Vaults are arch-like structures that are held together by the pressure of the stones that make up the arch.

_____ The impressive facade of the wall housing the main entrance of a mediaeval church. With the towers on either side and a great deal of sculptural detail and carving on the surface, it has a very imposing effect.

_____ A Gothic church showing a ribbed vault. This innovation meant a lighter roof, thus allowing for a taller building with thinner walls and more windows.

_____ The facade of a church illustrating the decorative windows. With the increased amount of space for glass, stained glass artists developed the rose window.

_____ An illustration of a rose window, a huge round window whose divisions look like the petals of a rose. These windows depict religious stories, often representing the Virgin Mary, the Mother of Christ.

Secular architecture consisted mainly of castles and fortresses built by kings or lords to defend their territory. In the Art Gallery, find an illustration that matches each description below.

_____ Ruins of a mediaeval castle. The donjon or keep shown here was the strongest part of the castle and the place where everyone retired when the outer defences had given way.

_____ Narrow holes in the stone walls of a castle allowing archers to shoot down at their enemies while remaining protected.

Sculpture

Most Romanesque sculpture was incorporated into church architecture. Most sculptors of the time liked to decorate with scenes from the Bible and animals. In the Art Gallery, find an illustration that matches each description below.

_____ Sculpture decorating a column of a cathedral, representing Mary and the baby Jesus escaping on a donkey led by Joseph.

_____ Relief decorating the main door of a church and showing Christ surrounded by his apostles.

In the later Middle Ages, churches continued to be decorated with sculptural scenes and figures, and sculpture was still primarily architectural in nature. In the Art Gallery, find an illustration that matches each description below.

_____ West portal of Chartres Cathedral with the very ornate reliefs and statue-columns on each side of the door

_____ Statue-columns from Rheims Cathedral illustrating a full three-dimensional sculpture style.

_____ The Bamberg rider was the first European example of a freestanding statue since the time of the Romans.

Painting and Decorative Arts

The decorative arts were important in the Middle Ages. Their beauty often served religious purposes. In the Art Gallery, find an illustration that matches each description below.

_____ Manuscripts were often embellished with paintings. This illuminated capital letter is illustrated with a biblical scene.

_____ Metalwork was a well-developed art form in the early Middle Ages. This reliquary is a receptacle built to hold the relics of a saint.

_____ Tapestries were important works of textile art. The Bayeux Tapestry is an embroidered illustration of the conquest of England by William, Duke of Normandy.

_____ Picture from a small book of prayers, *Les Très Riches Heures du Duc de Berry*, done by two manuscript artists, the Limbourg Brothers.

The Arts in the Middle Ages

Painting and Decorative Arts

The Gothic paintings of the later Middle Ages began to show the influence of the pre-Renaissance artists. They have a different sense of space and seem less two dimensional. In the Art Gallery, find an illustration that matches each description below.

_____ Fresco of *The Lamentation of Christ* by Giotto, a fourteenth-century Italian painter who rejected the traditional flat, two-dimensional style of the time.

_____ *Arnolfini and his Wife* by the Flemish painter Jan van Eyck, whose work bridges the gap between mediaeval art and that of the Renaissance. His works are much more naturalistic and his portraits express genuine personality.

The Madonna, or Virgin Mary, was an important subject of paintings in the mediaeval period. In the Art Gallery, find two representations of the Madonna and identify which one belongs to each description below.

_____ *Madonna Enthroned* by Duccio. This painting is typical of the Middle Ages with flat, stylized figures.

_____ *Madonna* (detail) by Jan van Eyck shows human figures that look much more like real people. This painting is much closer to the Renaissance style.

Musical Life in the Middle Ages

The Church

In the Middle Ages, most musicians worked for the Church.

Describe the use of music and the need for musicians in cathedrals.	Describe the use of music and the need for musicians in monasteries.

The Courts

There was also music outside the Church at the court.

Describe the use of music and the need for musicians at the court.	Describe the differences between the court poet-musician and the minstrels.
Name the three types of court poet-composers and indicate to which geographical region each group belongs:	Name one aristocrat who was very well known as a patron of the arts: Name two well-known aristocrats that were also poet-composers:

5

Music in the Middle Ages

Musical Notations

Musical notation was developed during the Middle Ages.

Name the first type of notation made up of simple little signs suggesting whether the voice should rise or fall: _____

Name the Italian monk who in the eleventh century developed the four-lined staff that made it possible to establish the relationship of one pitch to another: _____

The same monk invented a system of designating the notes of the scale with syllables. Where do the syllables ut, re, mi, fa, sol, la come from? _____

Name the notation that was developed in the twelfth century from the early signs, becoming separate notes indicated by broad horizontal lines, diamond-shaped dots and thin vertical lines: _____

By the thirteenth century, the time values for the different shapes were set down. This system lasted until the sixteenth century, then the shapes were changed to what? _____

Specific features

Among the following statements, identify (√) the ones that apply to plainsong.

_____ Vocal music written for the choirs found at all cathedrals and monasteries
_____ Instrumental music used to accompany the religious services in cathedrals and monasteries

_____ Has no regular beat or accent and tends to follow the rhythm of the text
_____ Strongly regulated rhythm with clear cadential points

_____ Made up of two or three lines of melody going on at the same time
_____ Only one melodic line sung by a single person or by a whole choir

_____ A tranquil, celestial stream of sound
_____ Energetic, lively and well-articulated musical lines

_____ About 3,000 chants are left to us
_____ As few as 100 chants are left to us

Among the following statements, identify (√) the elements that apply to secular songs.

_____ Written in Latin, the official language of the Church
_____ Written in the vernacular, i.e., the ordinary language of the people

_____ Typically, lyrical love songs written to the noble ladies of the court or songs portraying various aspects of ordinary life
_____ Lyrical songs based almost entirely on religious subjects

_____ No strict musical forms
_____ Based on musical forms closely related to the poetic structure of the verse forms

_____ About 300 troubadour songs and 1,400 trouvère songs are left to us
_____ About 2,000 troubadour songs and 3,000 trouvère songs are left to us

Specific features

Music in the Middle Ages

The tenth and eleventh centuries are marked by one of the most important developments in Western music, the evolution of polyphony.

Match each illustration with a description below:

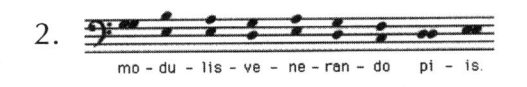

1. [musical notation: (Al-)le- (luia)]

2. [musical notation: mo- du- lis- ve- ne- ran- do pi- is.]

3. [musical notation: O Vir- go pi- a, Can- dens li- li- um / Lis ni glay Ni ro- sier fleu- ri,]

4. [musical notation]

5. [musical notation: [Solo] Hec]

_____ Earliest form of polyphony called organum. It consisted of a second line of melody added to a plainsong chant. To begin with, the two melodies ran parallel to one another, the notes of the second part a fourth or fifth below the first.

_____ A later development of organum where the second melody became more independent, showing contrary movement.

_____ Next stage of polyphony, in which the second voice began to sing several notes to each single chant note, and the chant notes were held for a long time, like drones.

_____ A new form of organum developed at the Cathedral of Notre Dame in Paris by Léonin and Pérotin, where a third voice is added to the polyphony. Definite rhythms were introduced and the different voices could each have a different rhythmic pattern.

_____ The motet is a more complex form of polyphony where words have been added to the upper voices of a three-part work. While the bottom voice consists of a piece of Gregorian chant in Latin set to a specific rhythm, the middle voice, the duplum, and the top voice, the triplum, were set to completely different texts, and were rhythmically much more complex.

Instrumental Music

Although vocal music played a central role in the Middle Ages, by the 1300s instrumental music was increasingly popular. Explain what instrumental music was used for:

_____
_____
_____
_____
_____
_____

Music in the Middle Ages

Instrumental Music

Early instruments fall into the same general groupings as modern ones. Name a few instruments for each category:	
String instruments that were plucked	
String instruments that were bowed	
Woodwind instruments played indoors	
Woodwind instruments played outdoors	
Woodwind instruments played indoors and outdoors	
Percussion instruments	
Name two kinds of keyboard instruments	

Religious composers

Much liturgical music of the Middle Ages has come down to us marked Anonymous, meaning we do not know who the composer was. But there are some composers whose names are known.

Name a woman composer of the early Middle Ages. She was a prioress of an important monastery and a powerful woman in her time. She wrote a large quantity of monophonic plainsong. _____

Name a master of music at the Cathedral of Notre Dame in Paris in the twelfth century. He is credited with developing organum and he is believed to be the author of *The Great Book of Organum*. _____

Name another master of music at the Cathedral of Notre Dame who was responsible for introducing definite rhythm patterns in the different organum parts. He is known to have composed at least two four-part works. _____

Troubadours and trouvères

We know the names and some of the music of these poet-composers.

Name one of the earliest troubadours from Aquitaine, grandfather of Eleanor of Aquitaine. _____

Name a well-known trouvère, son of Henry II of England and Eleanor of Aquitaine. He is best remembered as a crusader and for taking back the crown of England from his brother John. _____

Name a trouvère whose most famous work, *Le Jeu de Robin and Marion*, a secular drama, is regarded as a precursor of French comic opera. _____

Ars Nova composers

In fourteenth century France, a new style of music arose, which was much more complex and opened many new possibilities for composers.

Name one of the earliest important promoters of the Ars Nova. He is the author of the music theory text from which the movement got its name, in which he explained the new theories of notation and introduced symbols for new note durations. He was important in the development of the motet. _____

Name one of the most outstanding composers of the Ars Nova, whose complete works are preserved in a series of illuminated manuscripts. He is best known for his *Mass of Notre Dame*, one of the earliest polyphonic mass settings, but most of his music is secular. _____

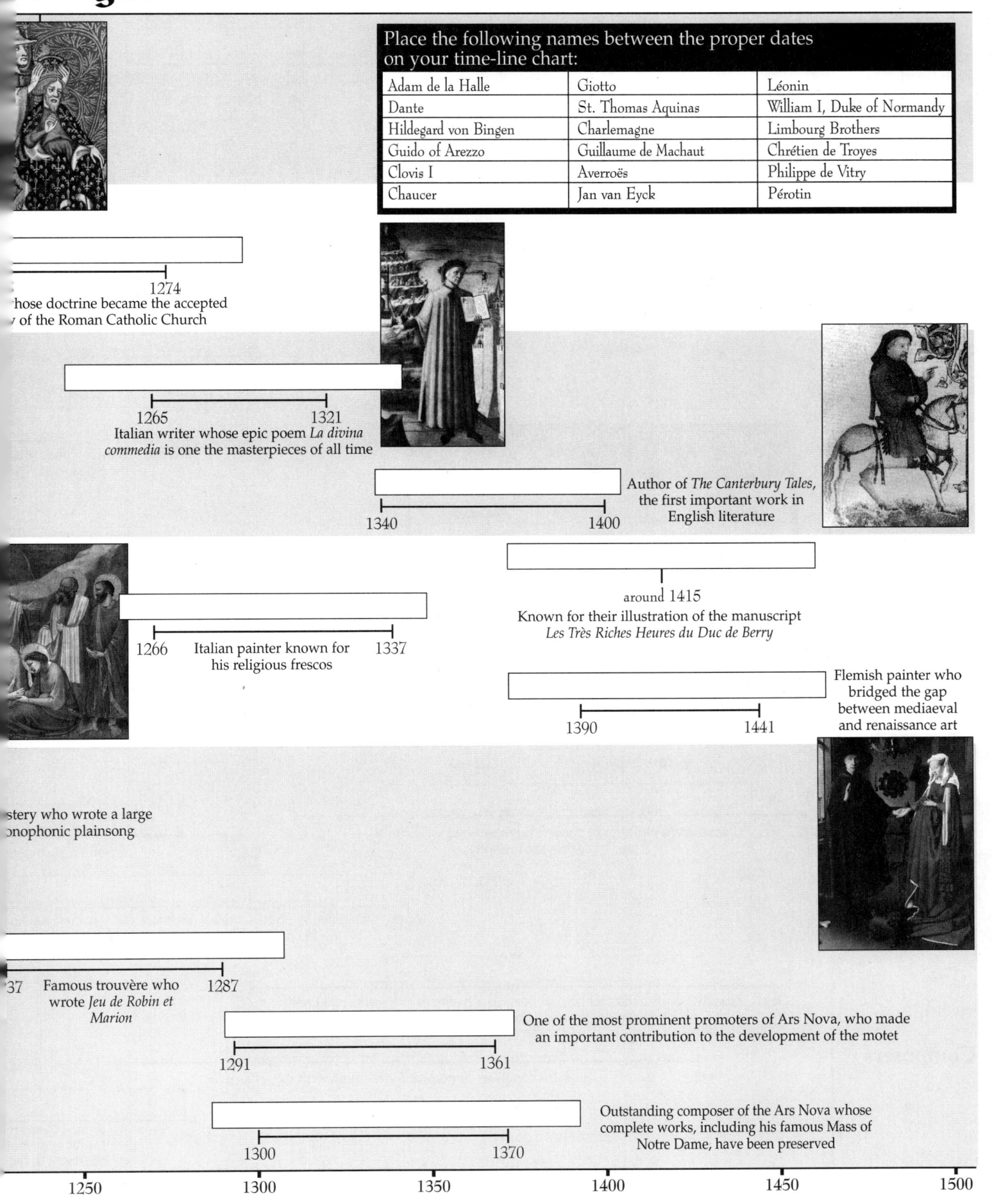

Middle Ages

Place the following names between the proper dates on your time-line chart:

Adam de la Halle	Giotto	Léonin
Dante	St. Thomas Aquinas	William I, Duke of Normandy
Hildegard von Bingen	Charlemagne	Limbourg Brothers
Guido of Arezzo	Guillaume de Machaut	Chrétien de Troyes
Clovis I	Averroës	Philippe de Vitry
Chaucer	Jan van Eyck	Pérotin

|—1274
whose doctrine became the accepted
of the Roman Catholic Church

|—1265———————1321|
Italian writer whose epic poem *La divina commedia* is one the masterpieces of all time

|—1340———————1400|
Author of *The Canterbury Tales*, the first important work in English literature

around 1415
Known for their illustration of the manuscript *Les Très Riches Heures du Duc de Berry*

|—1266———————1337|
Italian painter known for his religious frescos

|—1390———————1441|
Flemish painter who bridged the gap between mediaeval and renaissance art

stery who wrote a large
onophonic plainsong

37 |—————1287|
Famous trouvère who wrote *Jeu de Robin et Marion*

|—1291———————1361|
One of the most prominent promoters of Ars Nova, who made an important contribution to the development of the motet

|—1300———————1370|
Outstanding composer of the Ars Nova whose complete works, including his famous Mass of Notre Dame, have been preserved

1250   1300   1350   1400   1450   1500

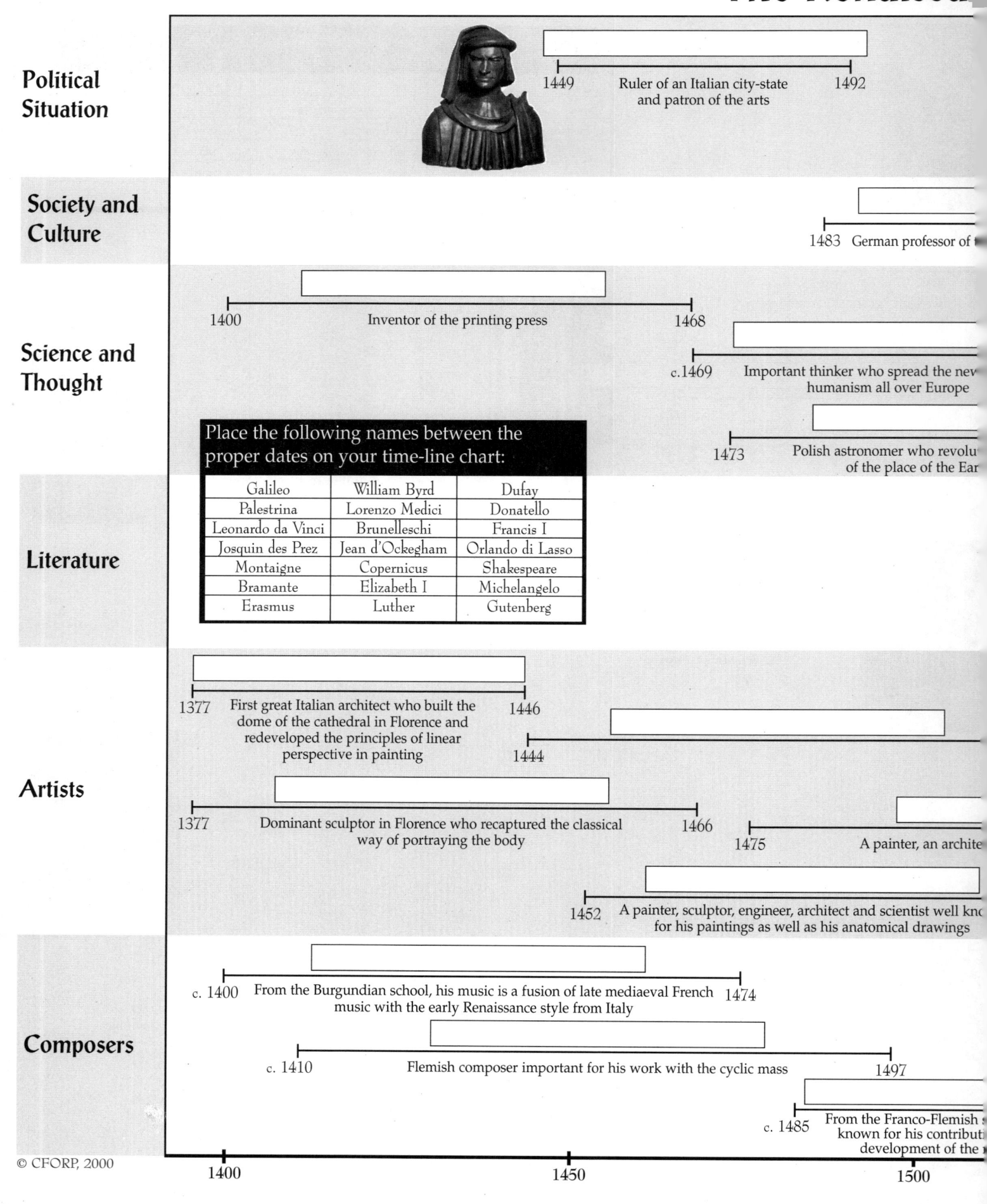

The Renaissance

Political Situation

1449 — Ruler of an Italian city-state and patron of the arts — 1492

Society and Culture

1483 German professor of...

Science and Thought

1400 — Inventor of the printing press — 1468

c.1469 — Important thinker who spread the new humanism all over Europe

1473 — Polish astronomer who revolu... of the place of the Ear...

Literature

Place the following names between the proper dates on your time-line chart:

Galileo	William Byrd	Dufay
Palestrina	Lorenzo Medici	Donatello
Leonardo da Vinci	Brunelleschi	Francis I
Josquin des Prez	Jean d'Ockegham	Orlando di Lasso
Montaigne	Copernicus	Shakespeare
Bramante	Elizabeth I	Michelangelo
Erasmus	Luther	Gutenberg

Artists

1377 — First great Italian architect who built the dome of the cathedral in Florence and redeveloped the principles of linear perspective in painting — 1446

1444

1377 — Dominant sculptor in Florence who recaptured the classical way of portraying the body — 1466

1475 — A painter, an archite...

1452 — A painter, sculptor, engineer, architect and scientist well kno... for his paintings as well as his anatomical drawings

Composers

c. 1400 — From the Burgundian school, his music is a fusion of late mediaeval French music with the early Renaissance style from Italy — 1474

c. 1410 — Flemish composer important for his work with the cyclic mass — 1497

c. 1485 — From the Franco-Flemish s... known for his contributi... development of the...

© CFORP, 2000

1400   1450   1500

Art Gallery
The Renaissance

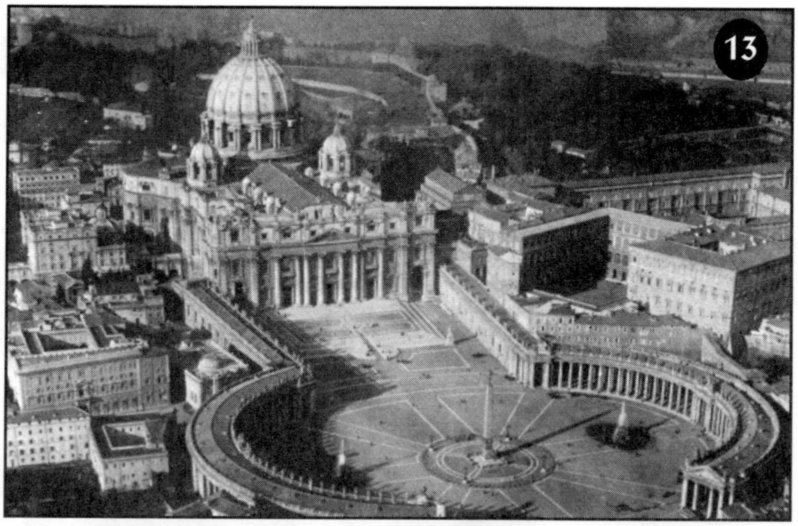
13

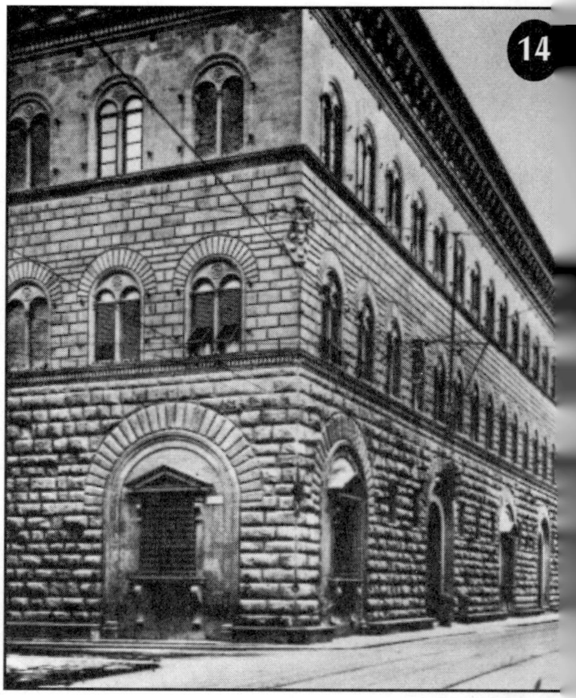
14

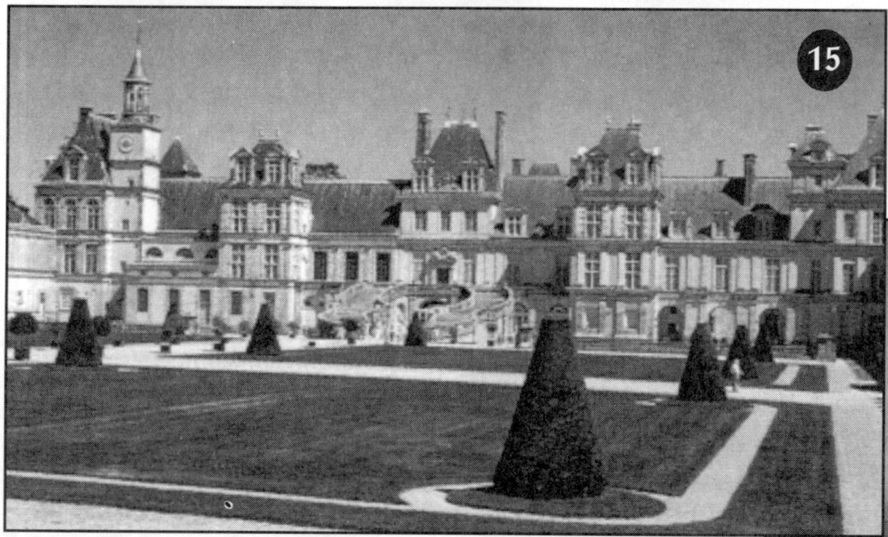
15

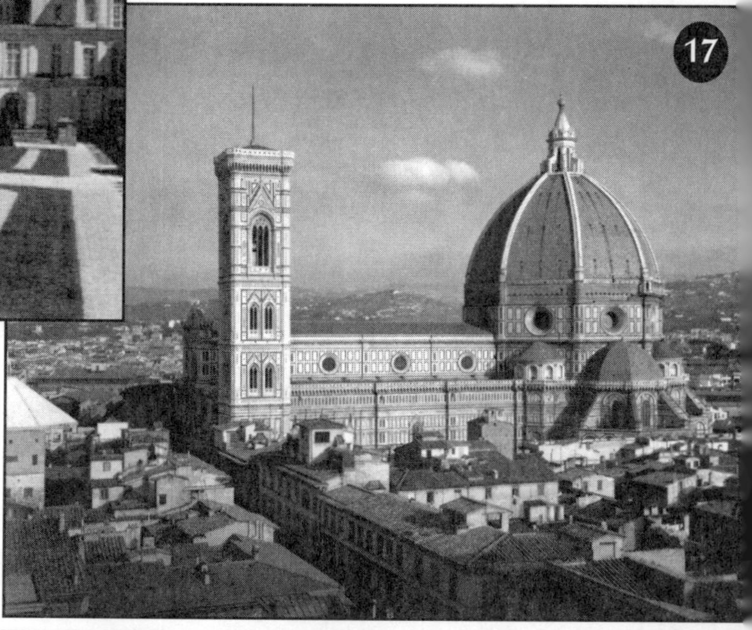
17

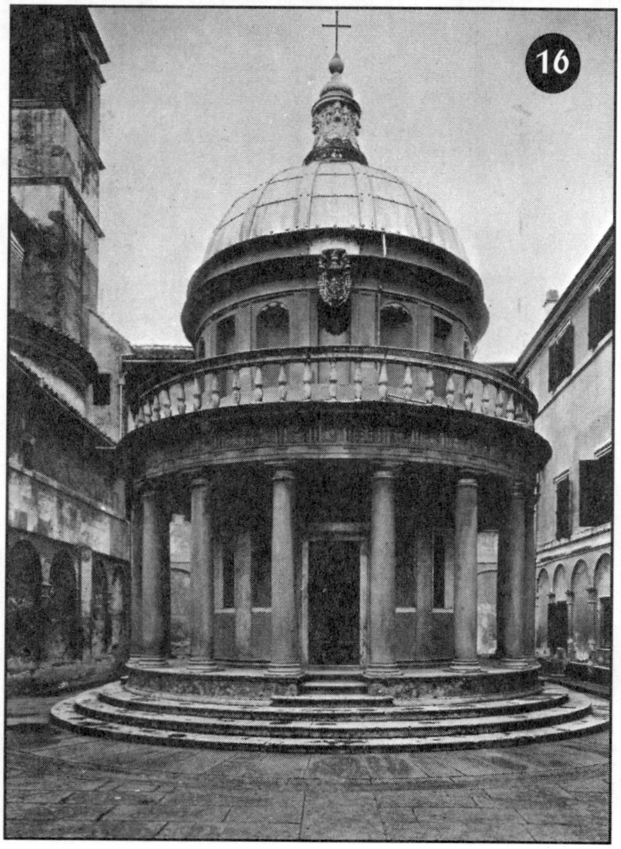
16

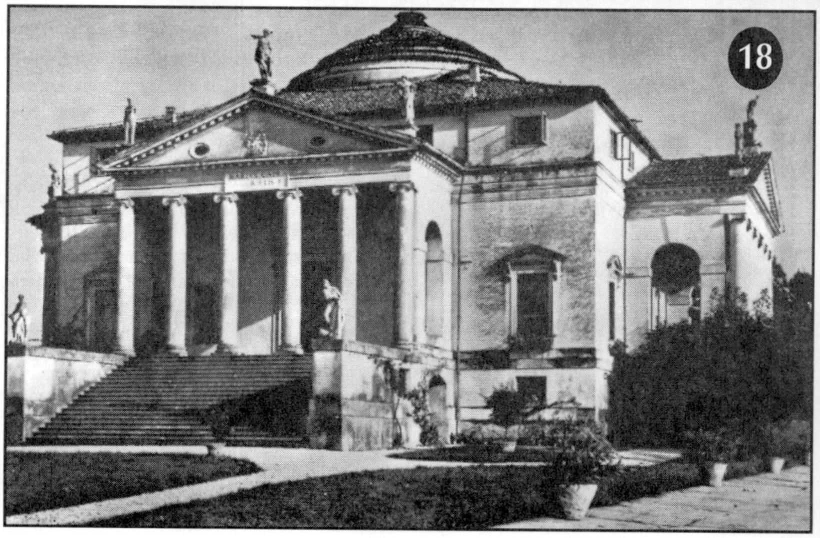
18

© CFORP, 2000

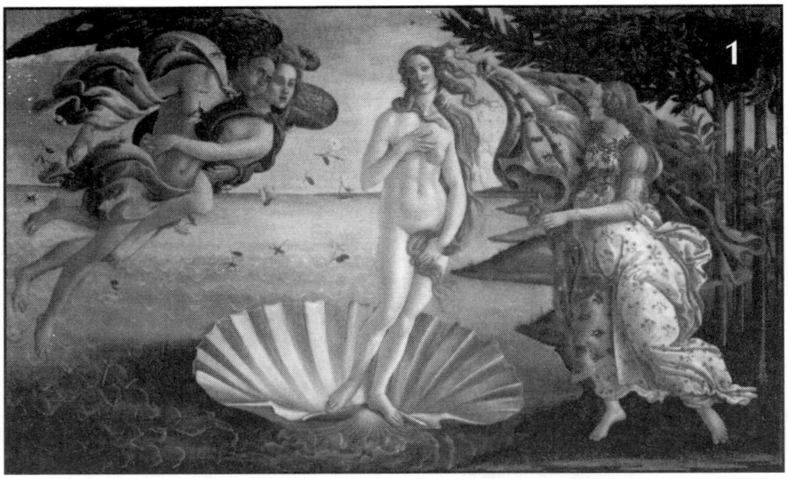
1

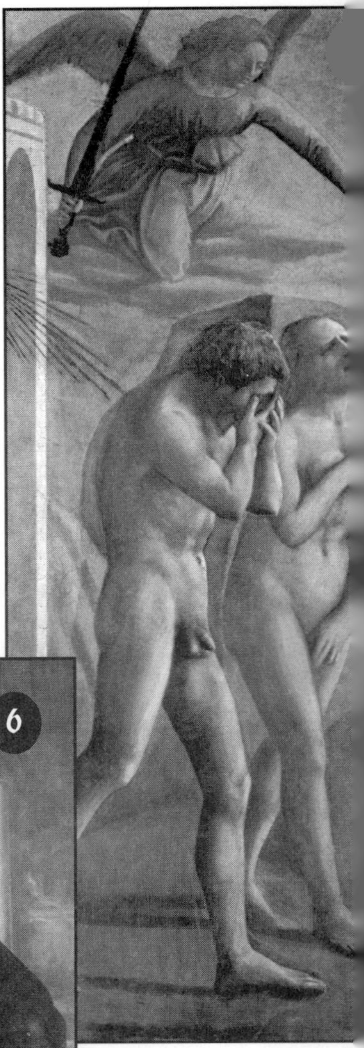

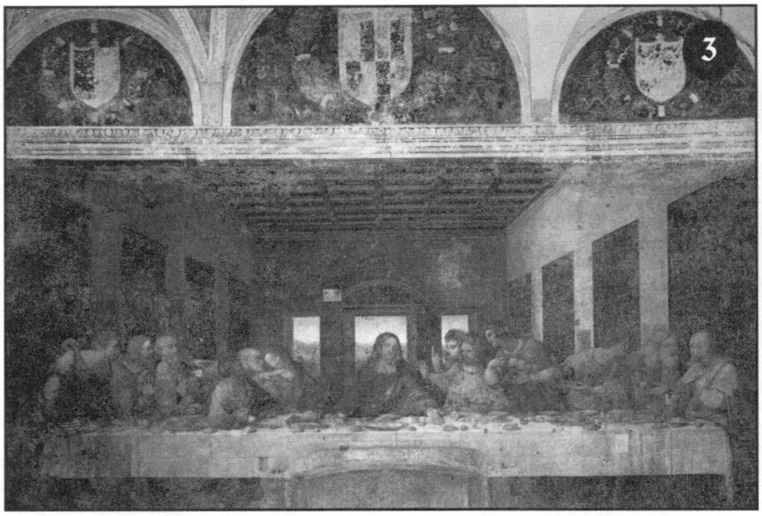
3

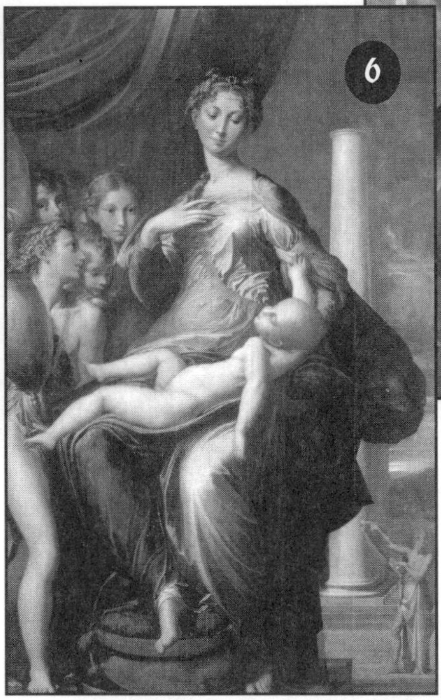
6

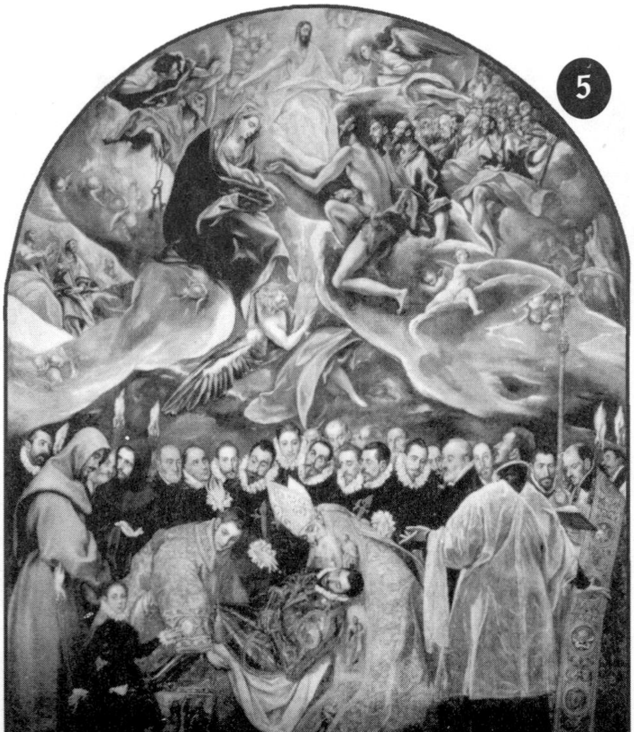
5

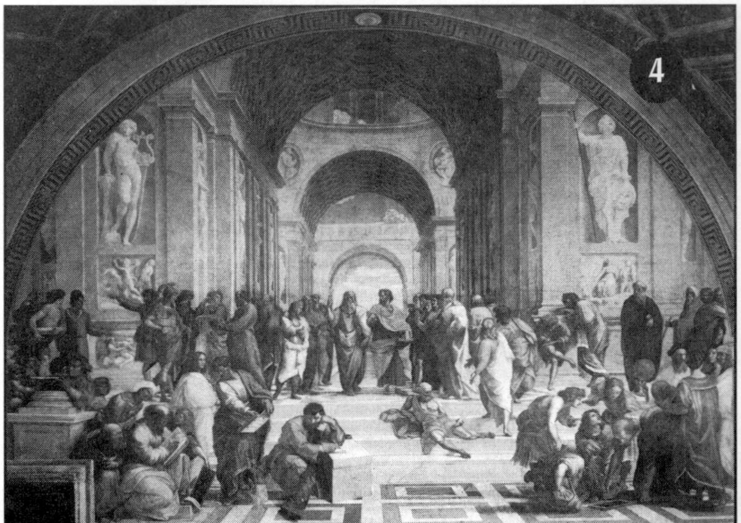
4

(1450-1600)

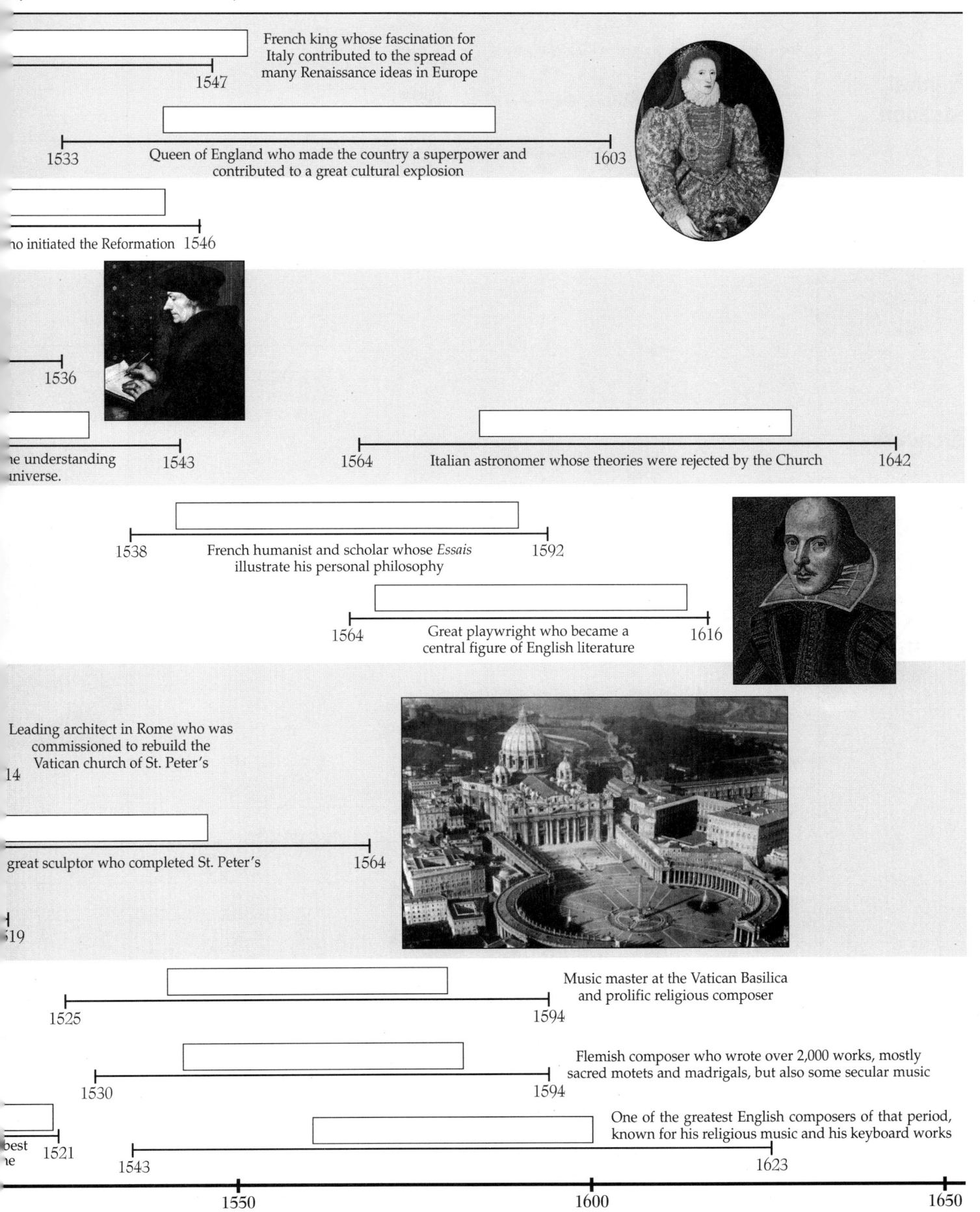

—1547	French king whose fascination for Italy contributed to the spread of many Renaissance ideas in Europe
1533—1603	Queen of England who made the country a superpower and contributed to a great cultural explosion
—1546	who initiated the Reformation
1536	
1543	the understanding universe.
1564—1642	Italian astronomer whose theories were rejected by the Church
1538—1592	French humanist and scholar whose *Essais* illustrate his personal philosophy
1564—1616	Great playwright who became a central figure of English literature
14—	Leading architect in Rome who was commissioned to rebuild the Vatican church of St. Peter's
—1564	great sculptor who completed St. Peter's
19	
1525—1594	Music master at the Vatican Basilica and prolific religious composer
1530—1594	Flemish composer who wrote over 2,000 works, mostly sacred motets and madrigals, but also some secular music
1521 best	
1543—1623	One of the greatest English composers of that period, known for his religious music and his keyboard works

1550 1600 1650

The M

Political Situation

465 – 511 : Considered the first King of France

747 – 814 : King of the Franks and Emperor of the Romans

1028 – 1087 : Norman noble who was crowned King of England

Thought

1126 — 1198
Muslim philosopher and physician whose analysis of the works of the Greek philosopher Aristotle influenced Christian philosophers.

Phi

Literature

1135 — 1183
Famous French poet who wrote about chivalry and courtly love

Artists

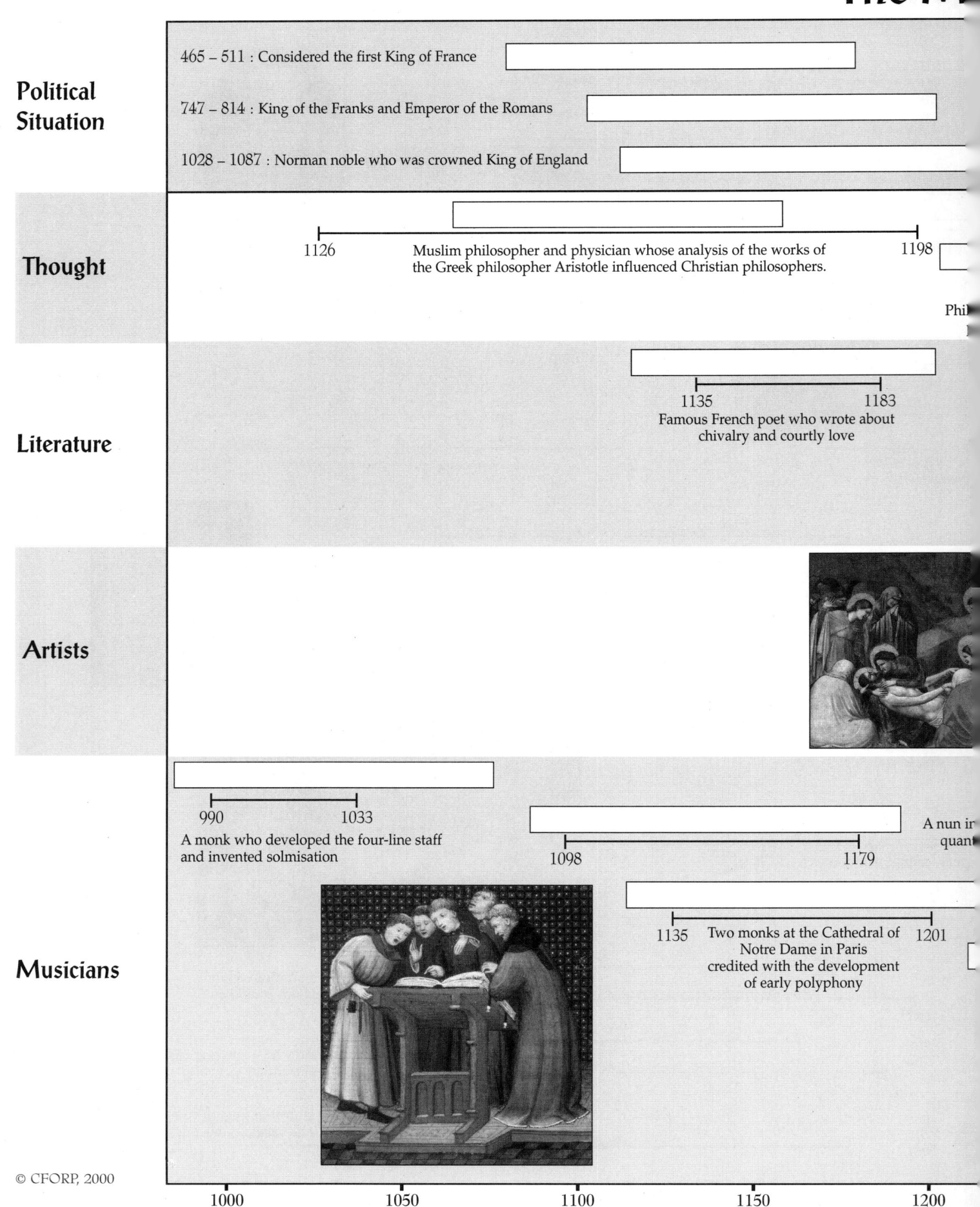

Musicians

990 — 1033
A monk who developed the four-line staff and invented solmisation

1098 — 1179
A nun i
quan

1135 — 1201
Two monks at the Cathedral of Notre Dame in Paris credited with the development of early polyphony

© CFORP, 2000

1000 1050 1100 1150 1200

The Political Situation — Life in the Renaissance

By the middle of the fifteenth century, northern Italy was divided into city-states. Name the four most powerful and influential cities: _____ , _____ , _____ , _____ .

Much of the cultural growth that occurred in the Italian Renaissance came as a result of the powerful families that ran the important city states. Name one of the most powerful families in Italy, who ruled Florence for a number of years and were patrons of writers and artists: _____ .

Name one well-known member of this family who, among other things, is remembered for having been the patron of Michelangelo and Botticelli: _____ .

Name other Italian ruling families who were involved in supporting artists and scholars:
_____
_____

Name the French King of the early sixteenth century who was fascinated with Italy and was responsible for the spread of many Renaissance ideas into France and the rest of Europe: _____ .

Name the King and Queen of Spain who, through marriage, united the two Spanish kingdoms: _____ and _____ .

Name the King of Spain who became the Holy Roman Emperor, thus controlling more territory than any other ruler in Europe: _____ .

Name the King of England who established the Church of England and who was responsible for the growth of Parliament and the House of Commons: _____ .

Name the Queen of England who brought stability to the country, made peace with France and encouraged trade, establishing England as a superpower: _____ .

Society and Culture

Give the name of the major event of the 1500s that ended the pan-European supremacy of the Pope in Rome and resulted in the birth of Protestantism, a new form of Christianity: _____ .

Name the German monk and professor of theology who initiated these major changes: _____ .

The late fifteenth and the sixteenth century was an intense period of exploration.

Name one of the most famous seafarers who sailed into unknown territory and discovered the New World:	
Name the seafarer who found a way to go to India by sailing around the African coast:	
Name the first explorer and navigator whose vessels sailed completely around the world:	
Name the English adventurer who sailed to Labrador, Newfoundland and New England:	
Name the French explorer who made two trips to North America thus laying the basis for the French empire in the New World:	

Life in the Renaissance

Science and Thought

With the invention of the printing press, books were no longer just available to the clergy or the aristocracy, but were able to reach a much broader public. Name the inventor of the printing press that could produce up to 300 copies a day: _____.

What was the first complete printed book? _____.

Renaissance humanism refers to the study of ancient literature, history and moral philosophy.

Classical works were already studied in the Middle Ages, but what was the main difference in the Renaissance?	
Enumerate the subjects that were part of the humanist education program:	
Explain the main focus of humanism.	

Name one of the most important humanist thinkers who lectured all over Western Europe and proposed enlightened views about children's education: _____.

Name his most famous work: _____.

Name a political philosopher who was preoccupied with the ideal leader and the methods of gaining and holding power: _____.

Name his most famous work: _____.

Name a Polish astronomer whose work *On the Revolution of the Celestial Spheres* changed the astronomical ideas of the time: _____.

Explain his main theory:

_____

_____

_____

Name an Italian astronomer who began to build telescopes and whose new discoveries were seen by the Church as heresy and were censored, forcing this scientist to renounce his theories: _____.

Literature — The Arts in the Renaissance

The reign of Elizabeth I saw the beginning of a golden age of English literature.

Name two English poets who developed English poetry style and form:
_____ and _____.

Drama was one of England's major contributions to world literature during the Renaissance.

Name the genius of the Elizabethan theatre who has been a dominant figure in literature for 400 years:	
List his best-known tragedies:	List his best-loved comedies:

Name an important French writer whose comic epics present humanist ideas: _____.
Name his two most famous works: _____ and _____.

Name a French humanist and scholar who wrote about his personal philosophy on many different matters:
_____. Name his best-known work: _____.

Name one of the earliest forms of professional theatre, which developed in Italy in the 1500s and spread to other countries: _____. Give the name of two of the most recognizable characters in this form of theatre: _____ and _____.

Architecture — Arts in the Renaissance

The architects of the Renaissance returned to the buildings of Greece and Rome for their inspiration. They applied classical design principles and built according to the mathematical proportions that had been declared harmonious in antiquity. Give the name of the architect that matches each description below.

	The first great Italian architect of the Renaissance who won the competition to complete the dome for the cathedral in Florence.
	A leading architect in Rome who received the commission to rebuild the Vatican church of St. Peter's.
	A multifaceted artist who brought the Vatican church to completion, incorporating his own ideas into the original plan.

In the Art Gallery, find an illustration that matches each description below.

	Brunelleschi's dome of the Cathedral in Florence
	Michelozzo's Medici Palazzo in Florence
	Bramante's Tempietto
	St. Peter's Basilica and the Vatican in Rome
	Palladio's Villa Rotunda
	French chateau of Fontainebleau

The Arts in the Renaissance

Sculpture

Give the name of the sculptor who matches each of the descriptions below.

	A dominant sculptor of the early Renaissance who worked primarily in Florence. He recaptured the classical way of portraying the body and his relief work, giving an illusion of depth, was innovative.
	A leading sculptor of the High Renaissance, and perhaps the best sculptor of all time. His greatest artistry is revealed in the works he carved from marble. He saw himself as a creator who was releasing the bodies he chiselled from their stone prisons.

In the Art Gallery, identify the following sculptures. For each one, give the name of the work and the name of the sculptor.

Art Work	Name of sculpture	Artist's name
19		
20		
21		
22		
23		

Painting

Renaissance painting is dramatically different from the painting of the Middle Ages.

List the characteristics of mediaeval paintings:	List the characteristics of Renaissance paintings:

| Painting | | The Arts in the Renaissance |

In the Art Gallery, identify the following frescoes or paintings. For each one, give the name of the work and the name of the artist who painted it.

Art Work	Name of fresco or painting	Artist's name
1		
2		
3		
4		
5		
6		
7		
8		
9		
10		
11		
12		

The painters of the Italian High Renaissance are some of the most famous artists in the history of the world. Identify the painters of this period by making a circle around their name.

A important Dutch painter was called the "creator of evils" because he populated his pictures with creatures who symbolized man's struggle with evil. Put a triangle beside the name of this painter.

The greatest Flemish painter of the 1500s is renowned for his landscapes and scenes of peasant life. He rejected the idealized figures of the Italian Renaissance in favour of realistic people in believable settings. Put a square beside the name of this painter.

A German painter and printmaker, who wanted to combine Italian theory with the native Northern interest in naturalistic detail, is best known for his woodcuts and engravings. Put a circle beside the name of this artist.

Musical Life in the Renaissance — Patrons and Musicians

The main patrons of music in the Renaissance remained, as they had been in the Middle Ages, the Church and the courts.

Name a few monarchs who were important patrons of the arts:	

Identify (√) the statements that are true.

With the rise of the city states in northern Italy and the changes of the Renaissance:	___ the demand for secular music increased with more opportunities for musicians to be employed as composers and performers
	___ the demand for secular music decreased and it was harder for musicians to find a job
Women working as professional musicians during the Renaissance:	___ were rare and tended to be singers or perhaps instrumentalists
	___ were fairly common and a lot of them were well respected composers
Amateur musicians during the Renaissance:	___ were fairly rare since very few people knew how to read music and only professional musicians could play an instrument, this ability being seen as a waste of time by the upper class and the merchant class
	___ became more and more common as the upper classes and the merchant classes learned how to read music, sing and play an instrument, these activities being seen as an important social accomplishment

Music in the Renaissance — General and Specific Features

Match each description to the appropriate musical features.

Paraphrase   Polychoral music   Musical borrowing   Word Painting   Imitation

	This technique involved having each voice in the music present the same musical phrase successively, so that as each line enters one after the other, the listener has the sense that the music overlaps.
	Musicians in Venice used antiphonal choirs, two or three choirs who answered each other alternately as well as singing together.
	Composers made use of existing plainsong melodies, well-known songs, and their own and other composer's works.
	[musical notation: Su- mens il- lud A- ve Ga-bri-e- lis o- re]
	Composers used a technique where the music matched the meaning of the word, contributing greatly to the emotional expressiveness of the music.

Identify (√) the statements that can be applied to harmony in the Renaissance.

___ Only fourths, fifths and octaves were considered as consonances

___ Thirds and sixths became acceptable consonances

___ Composers abandoned all sense of tonality for a freer style of writing

___ Composers developed the concept that a work begins with a definite keynote and returns to it again at the end, establishing a sense of tonality

___ By the end of the Renaissance period, writing in counterpoint lost its sway and composers often put more emphasis on one melodic line supported by chords

___ By the end of the Renaissance period, writing in counterpoint was the main composition style, and the concept of one melodic line supported by chords had not yet been developed

___ Composers worked exclusively with the ancient church modes and it was not until the next period, the Baroque era, that the major and minor systems gradually replaced the modal system

___ Composers were working more and more outside the ancient church modes, gradually reducing the number of modes to just major and minor, thus opening the way to the supremacy of tonality

Music in the Renaissance

Liturgical Forms

In liturgical forms, Renaissance composers concentrated their effort on unifying musically the five parts of the Mass called the Ordinary. By using the same original source for the different parts of the service, or by using similar imitative openings for all five sections, composers were trying to make the music of the Mass more of an organic whole. Give the name of the five parts of the Ordinary:

1. _____
2. _____
3. _____
4. _____
5. _____

Name the composer of each of these well-known masses:

Pope Marcellus Mass _____

Mass on L'homme armé _____

Missa Pange Lingua _____

Another important form of liturgical music was the motet. Give the characteristics of the Renaissance motet:

_____
_____
_____

Name the new musical forms for use in worship that appeared in Germany and England with the Reformation:

_____

Secular Forms

A type of secular song, the madrigal, developed in Italy then flourished in several European countries. Give the characteristics of the Renaissance madrigal:

Name the most important Italian madrigal composers:	Name the most important English madrigal composers:

Instrumental Music and Forms

In the Renaissance, composers began to write music to showcase instrumentalists and their talents, taking into account the capabilities and limitations of specific instruments.

Name the four main instruments or groups for which instrumental music was written:	1. _____ 3. _____ 2. _____ 4. _____
Renaissance dance music was generally composed in pairs contrasting in tempo and metre, but linked by the same melody. Give two examples of dance sets consisting of a slow dance followed by a faster one:	

Music in the Renaissance — Composers

In the Early Renaissance, the successive courts of the Dukes of Burgundy were known for the brilliance of their music. They attracted the leading musicians of the day.

Name a composer whose music is a fusion of late mediaeval French music with the early Renaissance style from Italy. He is said to have introduced the fauxbourdon and expanded the standard number of voices in a musical work to four.	

The Franco-Flemish school was the style of music that dominated European music in the last half of the fifteenth century. These musicians travelled all over Europe and served in many royal courts.

Name a Flemish composer, master of the canon technique, who is important for his work with the Mass, based on the concept that the different parts of the Ordinary should be pulled together with the use of one melody or chant.	
Name the composer who was considered by his peers as the greatest musician of his period, combining technical ingenuity with the ability to express emotion. Best known for his choral liturgical works, his main contribution was his development of the motet.	

Composers of the High Renaissance	
Name the Italian composer who was made music director for the Julian Chapel and master of music at the Vatican Basilica. He was asked to restore the plainsong then in use in the church to a more authentic style, but never completed this monumental task. He was a prolific composer whose style is noted for its balance, purity, control and clarity, and its emphasis on the integrity of the texts.	
Name a Flemish composer who was appointed music director at the important church of St. John Lateran in Rome, then was in charge of the chapel for the Duke of Bavaria. He wrote over 2,000 works, most of which were published during his lifetime. Many were sacred motets and madrigals, but he also wrote secular music in several international styles.	
Name a Spanish composer who wrote liturgical music almost exclusively and all his life was at the service of the Empress Maria, widow of the Holy Roman Emperor. He brought intense dramatic feeling to his music, a certain Spanish mysticism, and his harmonies were more chromatic than those of his contemporaries.	
Name two pre-eminent composers in Venice who were organists at St. Mark's Cathedral. They developed the concept of multiple choirs placed around the church producing a kind of "surround-sound" effect.	
Name one of the most important composers of English sacred music of the first half of the sixteenth century, who is responsible for introducing European-style polyphony to England.	
Name the greatest English composer of the latter half of the sixteenth century. He wrote music for both the Catholic and Protestant churches and is also known as a composer of keyboard works, whose many pieces for the virginal set the standard for later English composers.	
Name the first of the English madrigalists, whose style shows clarity of texture, sprightly rhythms and warm harmonies.	

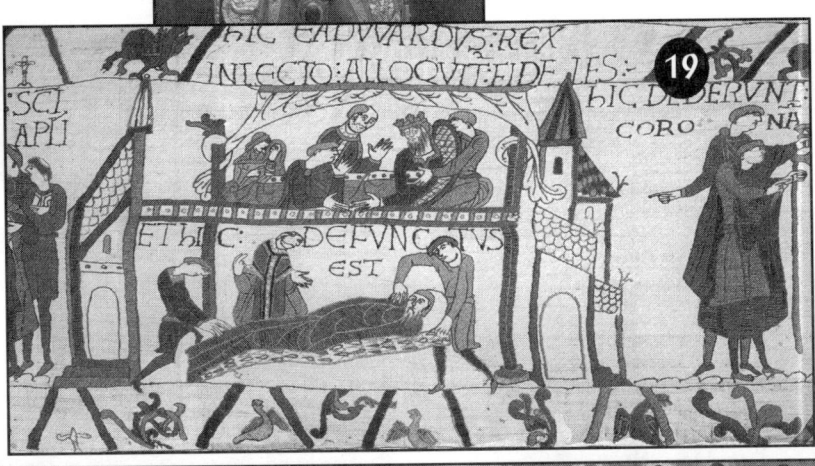

Authors: Gilles Comeau and Rosemary Covert
CFORP, 2000

Permission is given to reproduce the student activity book for classroom use only.

ISBN 2-89442-907-X
Copyright — second semester 2000
National Library of Canada

ISBN 2-89442-907-X

MUS-071-C1

9 782894 429075